111012

Work

Work

A KINGDOM PERSPECTIVE ON LABOR

Ben Witherington III

William B. Eerdmans Publishing Company

Grand Rapids, Michigan / Cambridge, U.K.

Published 2011 by
Wm. B. Eerdmans Publishing Co.
2140 Oak Industrial Drive N.E., Grand Rapids, Michigan 49505 /
P.O. Box 163, Cambridge CB3 9PU U.K.

Printed in the United States of America

17 16 15 14 13 12 11   7 6 5 4 3 2 1

Library of Congress Cataloging-in-Publication Data

Witherington, Ben, 1951-
  Work: a Kingdom perspective on labor / Ben Witherington III.
    p.   cm.
  ISBN 978-0-8028-6541-0 (pbk.: alk. paper)
  1. Work — Religious aspects — Christianity.   2. Work —
  Biblical teaching.   I. Title.

  BT738.5.W58   2011
  261.8′5 — dc22

                                                    2010040497

www.eerdmans.com

Contents

Caution — Work in Progress

I was leafing through a newspaper shortly before Thanksgiving and came across a political cartoon. It depicted two Indians carrying a dead turkey on a pole toward a table at which several New England Puritans were sitting, apparently waiting to eat their Thanksgiving dinner with the Natives. The Indians were far enough out of earshot not to be heard when one said to the other, "I don't care if they have a good work ethic, they are illegal aliens. They should go back to where they came from and enter the country legally and with our permission." I laughed for a good while about that reversal of the common perspective we hear in America today about so many illegal aliens. But the cartoon also alluded to something that it was assumed a broad audience would readily know all about — the so-called Puritan work ethic.

Christianity in general, and Protestant Christianity in particular, seems to raise to a peculiar degree the issue of how we should view work. Is it a blessing or a bane? Is it a duty or a privilege? Do we work to live, or live to work? Yet in spite of the stereotype of the Puritan work ethic, modern Americans, including many Christians, have little or no understanding of what the Bible actually says about work, and it hardly informs their views on questions of work versus play, or career versus retirement, or other related subjects. And in one sense, they can hardly be blamed — Christian theologians have seldom addressed the topic of work, which is what we intend to explore in this little study.

On Defining Work

In his recent study on work, David Jensen puts it this way: "[The] topic — human labor — is rather foreign to most systematic theologies. Not often have the codifiers of Christian doctrine explored the topic of work as an explicitly theological theme."[1] If you survey the topical indexes in works of biblical and systematic theology you will find the topic *work* rarely — because it is rarely discussed in the text of such books! How odd, especially when the Bible has so much to say about work, past, present, and future. Consider Jensen's helpful summary:

> Biblical narratives overflow with work. Between the opening lines of Genesis, which portray God as a worker, and the closing chapter of Revelation, with a vision of new creation, God labors. One of the distinguishing characteristics of biblical faith is that God does not sit enthroned in heaven removed from work, willing things into existence by divine fiat. Unlike the gods of the Greco-Roman mythologies, who absolve themselves of work [or make work a punishment for troublesome persons, e.g., Sisyphus] dining on nectar and ambrosia in heavenly rest and contemplation — the biblical God works.[2]

But the Bible is by no means just about God working; it is also about God's people working, and about their participation in work that God sees as good, endorses, and indeed participates in.

---

1. D. H. Jensen, *Responsive Labor: A Theology of Work* (Louisville: Westminster John Knox, 2006), p. x.
2. Jensen, *Responsive Labor*, p. 22.

Perhaps part of the problem is that we have never bothered to ask and answer the question — *what is work?* — from a biblical point of view. This is strange when we have so many workaholics in our culture, individuals who live to work, rather than work to live. Many economists would reduce the definition of work to the lowest common denominator — *whatever we do to live or survive.* The problem with this definition is not merely that it is too broad. (After all, running from an oncoming attacker or swerving to avoid a car accident is something you do to survive, but neither is what we would call work. Likewise, eating and sleeping are not work, even though we do them in order to survive and thrive.) Rather, the problem is that it has no theological component.

I like Frederick Buechner's definition of work: "The place where your deep gladness meets the world's deep need."[3] The problem with this definition is that one may stop after reading the first half. It is entirely possible to take delight in making something that the world hardly needs, like the man who made the world's largest ball of tinfoil, collecting, combining, and toiling over many years on his pet project. Of course, Buechner's full definition stresses that work comes at the intersection of delight and *need.*

It is always rewarding to know you are doing something that helps others, and very rewarding if you know you are doing something that is so purposeful it saves lives. But regardless of whether you take delight in it, if it meets genuine and crucial needs in the world, it is good work and should be done. Buechner is suggesting that deep inside we are made for work, and when we find our calling, purpose, vocation, or ministry it will bring deep satisfaction when we do it. I can attest to this truth myself. I love preaching, teaching, and writing. It's hard for me to imagine my adult life without doing one or more of these things. These tasks bring me

3. F. Buechner, *Wishful Thinking: A Seeker's ABC* (San Francisco: Harper, 1993), p. 119.

great joy and hopefully bring others some considerable benefit. But at the end of the day Buechner's definition seems to focus too much on our personal fulfillment to be fully adequate.

David Jensen settles for a definition of work that has a theological component. Work, he says, is any activity undertaken with a sense of obligation to self, others, one's community, or one's God.[4] The problem I have with this definition is that *all activities* that a Christian undertakes should fall under that last rubric. By this I mean all work should be seen as part of the obligations placed on us by God, whatever else may also be the case, and all work must be doable as something that glorifies God and edifies others. This is precisely why, for example, I would say it is entirely debatable whether war can be called legitimate work from a Christian point of view — that is, if the Sermon on the Mount is supposed to describe how the disciple of Jesus is to live, work, and behave.

Another attempt at defining work is made by Miroslav Volf. He suggests, "Work is honest, purposeful, and methodologically specified social activity whose primary goal is the creation of products or states of affairs that can satisfy the needs of working individuals or their co-creatures, or (if primarily an end in itself) activity that is necessary in order for acting individuals to satisfy their needs apart from the need for the activity itself."[5] In this definition, leisure is contrasted with work, but of course that still leaves a host of activities that do not seem to naturally fall into either the category of leisure or work — eating and sleeping, for example, or even just breathing. Notice, however, the close connection between work and its purpose — to satisfy human needs (what sort is not specified).

What I find especially unsatisfactory about this definition is its basically a-theological character. Volf's real stress is on work as

4. Jensen, *Responsive Labor*, p. 3.
5. M. Volf, *Work in the Spirit: Toward a Theology of Work* (Eugene, Ore.: Wipf and Stock, 2001), pp. 10-11.

a means to an end, namely, the meeting of human needs. In this way he can distinguish work from hobbies. But in fact the activity undertaken as work can also be undertaken as hobby, and in both cases be a means to an end which is extrinsic to the worker's need to do it. For instance, if I love building computers and I make one for my son as a birthday present, knowing that he needs a computer for work, I have made it as a gift for his birthday. I could have gone out and bought one with the same result. My labor was not compulsory to meet the need. And yet, just because I exercise my skills in something I love to do (and do not do as part of my "job"), this does not prevent what I am doing from being classified as either a hobby activity, or work, or both! Nevertheless, Volf is absolutely right when he stresses that a Christian theology of work will not be sufficient if it is based almost entirely on the creation theology of the Old Testament.

It will perhaps surprise you to discover how little theologians have actually discussed work. In fact the first modern, full-dress theology of work does not seem to have been written until the 1950s, which I find astounding considering how much of our waking hours are consumed by work.[6] In any case, the coming of Christ has changed the eschatological situation. Volf puts it this way: "Christian life is life in the Spirit of the new creation or it is not Christian life at all. And the Spirit of God should determine the whole life, spiritual as well as secular, of a Christian. Christian work must, therefore, be done under the inspiration of the Spirit and in the light of the coming new creation."[7] Now we are getting somewhere! And right away there seems to be a clear implication — work that the Holy Spirit would never inspire should never be done by a Christian — say, for example, creating pornography, to take an easy example.

The Holy Spirit's inspiration of work automatically comes

6. See Volf, *Work in the Spirit,* p. 71.
7. Volf, *Work in the Spirit,* p. 79.

with an ethical component. The works of the flesh are not the works of the Spirit. We will say more on this. But it is not just that Christian work is Spirit-inspired and Spirit-enabled; it is that Christian work looks forward to the coming Kingdom on earth, the new creation; it does not merely live out of the old creation and its applicable rules. Thus, we could offer the following as a Christian definition of work: *any necessary and meaningful task that God calls and gifts a person to do and which can be undertaken to the glory of God and for the edification and aid of human beings, being inspired by the Spirit and foreshadowing the realities of the new creation.* To this we may add that any such work is worthy of fair remuneration, for "a workman is worthy of his hire" (1 Tim. 5:18).

A great deal of the problem we have in America in discussing our work is that our approach and attitudes about work are grounded in unbiblical myths of various kinds. Take, for example, the myth that our lives should involve a period of work, which, if done well, then entitles us to retirement, maybe even early retirement! Where exactly is the notion of retirement found in the Bible? Nowhere! Not even in the eschaton envisioned by the prophets do we have images of a workless paradise.

Work was part of the original creation design, and it appears to be in the works for the new creation as well. Work should be neither demonized nor divinized.[8] If we were to contrast for a moment, however, the creation and the eschatological visions of work in the Bible, we could say that in the creation accounts work is what human beings were fitted and commanded to do, whereas in the eschatological accounts it is what the Spirit inspires and gifts them to do, and in which they find joy. Work is inherent to

---

8. On the latter, compare Thomas Carlyle, who once claimed that work is "the latest Gospel in this world," a gospel that elevates humankind "from the low places of this Earth, very literally into divine Heavens." T. Carlyle, *Past and Present* (Boston: Riverside, 1965), p. 294. In a remarkable transformation of the monastic phrase *ora et labora*, Carlyle said, *labora est ora* — work is praying! (p. 196).

being created in God's image, for Genesis 1:26 tells us that we were created in God's image in order that we might have dominion over creation.

Consider for a moment a famous, and famously misused and misquoted, passage from Isaiah's vision of the final future:

> In days to come
>   the mountain of the LORD's house
> shall be established as the highest of the mountains,
>   and shall be raised above the hills;
> all the nations shall stream to it.
>   Many peoples shall come and say,
> "Come, let us go up to the mountain of the LORD,
>   to the house of the God of Jacob;
> that he may teach us his ways
>   and that we may walk in his paths."
> For out of Zion shall go forth instruction,
>   and the word of the LORD from Jerusalem.
> He shall judge between the nations,
>   and shall arbitrate for many peoples;
> *they shall beat their swords into plowshares,*
>   *and their spears into pruning hooks;*
> *nation shall not lift up sword against nation,*
>   *neither shall they learn war any more.*
> *O house of Jacob,*
>   *come, let us walk*
>   *in the light of the LORD!* (2:2-5)

Our concern is particularly with the end of that quote, the part I have italicized. When Isaiah envisions the eschatological age, or the last days, he does not envision a massive work stoppage. What he envisions is a massive war stoppage, if we may put it that way. The point of beating swords into plowshares and spears into pruning hooks is so that the weapons of war may be turned into the tools of work. When Isaiah envisages the final or eschatological state of affairs, his vision of shalom, well-being, peace, is not of a workless paradise, but of a world at peace worshiping the one true God and working together rather than warring with each other. We see this very same sort of vision of the final future in Isaiah 65:20-25:

> No more shall there be in it
> > an infant that lives but a few days,
> > or an old person who does not live out a lifetime;
> for one who dies at a hundred years will be considered a
> > youth,
> > and one who falls short of a hundred will be considered
> > accursed.
> They shall build houses and inhabit them;
> > they shall plant vineyards and eat their fruit.
> They shall not build and another inhabit;
> > they shall not plant and another eat;
> for like the days of a tree shall the days of my people be,
> > and my chosen shall long enjoy the work of their hands.
> They shall not labor in vain,
> > or bear children for calamity;
> for they shall be offspring blessed by the LORD —
> > and their descendants as well.
> Before they call I will answer,
> > while they are yet speaking I will hear.
> The wolf and the lamb shall feed together,
> > the lion shall eat straw like the ox;
> > but the serpent — its food shall be dust!
> They shall not hurt or destroy
> > on all my holy mountain, says the LORD.

We could compare these two passages from Isaiah to Zechariah 8:10-12, where again paradise involves a war stoppage, not a work stoppage, so that crops can be sown and their fruit enjoyed in peace. Work apparently *isn't* the human dilemma; war and other sorts of fallen human behavior are.

It is no accident that Jesus in his inaugural sermon in Nazareth quotes the prophetic vision of Jubilee and suggests that his bringing of such prophecies to pass, his bringing in of the Kingdom, involves work — including the work of healing people. I agree with Volf when he says that a Christian definition of work must take into account where history is going in God's hands and thus "a theological interpretation of work is only valid if it facilitates transformation of work toward ever-greater correspondence with the coming new creation."[9]

Thus we must be constantly asking, Is this work that foreshadows the Kingdom and its ends and aims and character? The goal of human history, or at least its end, according to Revelation 21–22, is that God, humankind, and creation will finally be brought back into harmony, shalom, positive ongoing relationship. Our eschatology must shape our vision of our tasks.[10] These same passages envisage work continuing in the Kingdom. Thus we must not overemphasize the discontinuity between this age and the age to come, when it comes to work.

Presumably, whatever is true, and good, and beautiful in life and human culture will be cleansed of sin's taint and remain in the new creation. Nothing good will be wasted; we will not be laboring in vain. The inherent value and goodness of work will be upheld in the Kingdom, just as the inherent goodness and value of all creation will be upheld: "Creation itself . . . will be set free from its bondage to decay and obtain the glorious freedom of the children of God" (Rom. 8:21).

As many commentators have noticed, the vision of our final future in such prophetic passages as the ones we have cited or al-

9. Volf, *Work in the Spirit,* p. 83.
10. Volf, *Work in the Spirit,* p. 85.

luded to seems to be largely a reprise of the vision found in Genesis 2 — once a gardener, always a gardener. To use the old German theological terms, the *Endzeit* is like the original *Urzeit* in that there is no fallenness anymore, no shadow over the land, no laboring in vain, no winter without Christmas, as C. S. Lewis puts it in *The Lion, the Witch and the Wardrobe*. But there is laboring even in Paradise that came and is to come![11]

This raises some very serious questions about the whole notion of retirement either in this life or in the life to come. Is it even a biblical idea, or does it even comport with biblical ideas about our future, whether individually or collectively, when the Kingdom comes in full measure on earth? These are the sort of things we need to explore in this little book in some depth. But one more story first.

It was January 2009 and I was on sabbatical from Asbury Seminary, writing up in Vermont. I decided to take a morning and go to Weston Priory and spend some time in prayer. Most people's vision of monasteries is that they are places where there is a lot of prayer and worship and singing, but otherwise not much goes on and not much gets accomplished. This could hardly be more false.

The monks at Weston Priory follow the Benedictine rule of *Ora et Labora*, prayer and labor, or prayer and work, which includes making some wonderful maple syrup and cheese and engaging in all sorts of charitable activities. These monks are hardly resting on their laurels late in life, nor are they so heavenly minded that they have become no earthly good. Indeed, I would say they have the right perspective on things, for they know that the "work" of worship is the most important activity that tran-

11. One of the major problems with the extant exercises in biblical theology on the subject of work is that they work forward through the Bible, rather than backward, and the end result is that in most cases they never get to an eschatological or Kingdom perspective on work, that is, work in light of the inbreaking Kingdom, which is the contribution of this particular study.

spires on earth, the activity that most foreshadows both the nature of heaven and the future of the Kingdom on earth.[12]

As I was leaving the monastery I noticed a banner hanging just outside the little chapel. It quoted that great sage and prophet Jimi Hendrix, who once said, "When the power of love overcomes the love of power, the world will know peace." Well, the monks were working on the basis of that belief and so was Jesus. Notice, though: I used the word *working*. It's high time for us to begin contemplating the meaning of work from a more biblical, a more Kingdom point of view. Let this preface serve as our call to wake up and to get to work on rethinking work.

---

12. On which see my book, *We Have Seen His Glory: A Vision of Kingdom Worship* (Grand Rapids: Eerdmans, 2010).

CHAPTER ONE

An Opus That Is Magnum:
On the Goodness of Work

What is — "Paradise" —
Who live there —
Are they "Farmers" —
Do they "hoe" —
Do they know that this is "Amherst" —
And that I — am coming — too —

Emily Dickinson

Our England is a garden, and such gardens are not made
By singing: — "Oh, how beautiful!" and sitting in the shade.

Rudyard Kipling

Though Jesus stilled a storm, he didn't remove all storms from
the life of the world; though Jesus cured individuals of diseases,
he didn't rid the world of those diseases. To use the Gospel of
John's "sign" language, Jesus' actions point to a future world,
thereby signaling that the kind of world Isaiah envisioned is on

its way. Jesus provided signs of a different future that God has in store for the natural world.

Terence Fretheim[1]

A Creation and New Creation Perspective on Work

Somewhere along the line, Adam got a bad rap, or at least the God of Adam did. Someone somewhere misread the story of Creation and Fall and came to the conclusion that work was a result of the Fall, not part of God's original creation design for human beings. On closer inspection, it is perfectly clear that God's good plan always included human beings working, or, more specifically, living in the constant cycle of work and rest. Permanent rest was to come only when one was "gathered to one's fathers," to use the patriarchal term. Permanent rest was to come only when one had been interred and had an *R.I.P.* sign over one's head. Barbara Brown Taylor writes that many readers of Genesis 1–3 "have somehow gotten the idea that physical labor is part of God's curse — labor pains for the woman and field labor for the man — until labor itself gets all mixed up with punishment. Clearly, this is not so. The earthling's first divine job is to till the earth and keep it."[2]

Even just a momentary glance at the creation story tells us that work was meant to be in our DNA from the outset — God called humanity to fill the earth and subdue it. As Terence Fretheim has recently pointed out, the verb *subdue* in Genesis 1:28 indicates that even before the Fall, while the creation God made was "good," this does not mean it was tranquil and tame. There was a built-in wildness to it, and various kinds of inherent poten-

1. Fretheim, *Creation Untamed: The Bible, God, and Natural Disasters* (Grand Rapids: Baker Academic, 2010), p. 152.

2. B. Brown Taylor, *An Altar in the World: A Geography of Faith* (San Francisco: HarperOne, 2009), p. 151.

tial for growth and development.[3] Furthermore, there is no reason for us to think that subduing the world is supposed to be easy or idyllic. Think of the back-breaking, bone-wearying work of someone like Daniel Boone, trailblazing and subduing the Kentucky wilderness.[4] And here is where the Fall comes into the picture.

It is not work itself but the *toilsomeness* of work that was added to the equation as a result of the curse involved in the Fall. Both man and woman would experience "labor pains," indicates Genesis 3 — man in manipulating the good earth, woman in giving birth to children. But even here, what is said about the woman is that her pain in childbirth would be increased, which implies there was pain already inherent in the process of giving birth. Pain itself is not entirely a result of the Fall. In this case, "no pain, no childbirth" is what Genesis suggests. And there is another factor. Paul reminds us in Romans 8 that the whole of creation itself was subjected in the Fall, subject to futility, as he puts it, and therefore longs for liberation as much as we do.[5] The earth itself is not at its best and some of it is quite resistant to use or change, much less to subduing or tending.

But it's not just all about subduing an unruly and unruled earth. In fact, the earliest full images of human work and purpose are found in Genesis 2:15: "The LORD God took the man and put him in the garden of Eden to till it and keep it." The first profession for humans, it would appear, was gardening. "Here human work is shown to have worth and dignity as a service to God and as something that gives purpose to human life. Work here is a creation or-

3. Prof. Fretheim was kind enough to send me the draft of his 2010 Theta Phi Lecture given at Asbury Theological Seminary. This lecture has been incorporated into his book *Creation Untamed*.

4. See, for example, R. R. Morgan, *Boone: A Biography* (Chapel Hill: Algonquin, 2008).

5. I have spoken of the doxological character that work can have in my book, *We Have Seen His Glory: A Kingdom Perspective on Worship* (Grand Rapids: Eerdmans, 2010).

dinance, a God-appointed necessity for human life."[6] W. R. Forrester, in reflecting on Genesis 1–3, concludes, "Man was meant to be a gardener, but by reason of his sin he became a farmer."[7]

None of this, however, should lead us to the conclusion that good work, of whatever sort, is inherently futile or a result of the Fall. Indeed, even hard work, even hard manual labor is commended in the Scriptures, and sloth, as we shall see, is roundly condemned. In his crucial discussion of the matter Terence Fretheim makes the following key observation:

> Genesis does not present the creation as a finished product, wrapped up with a big red bow and handed over to the creatures to keep it exactly as originally created. It is not a one-time production. Indeed, for the creation to stay just as God originally created it would constitute a failure of the divine design. From God's perspective, the world needs work; development and change are what God intends for it, and God enlists human beings (and other creatures) to that end. From another angle, God did not exhaust the divine creativity in the first week of the world; God continues to create and uses creatures in a vocation that involves the becoming of creation.[8]

But my concern in this study is not merely to rehabilitate our notions of work by correcting bad exegesis of Genesis 1–3. My concern is to ask and answer the question of how work looks different in the light of Kingdom come, how work looks different if one believes Christ has changed the eschatological situation by his coming and that this affects the way we look at all we do as Christians.

The first thing to point out about the coming Kingdom is that

6. L. Ryken, "Work, Worker," in *The Dictionary of Biblical Imagery,* ed. L. Ryken, J. Wilhoit, and T. Longman III (Downers Grove: InterVarsity, 1998), p. 966.

7. W. R. Forrester, *Christian Vocation* (New York: Scribners, 1953), p. 130.

8. Fretheim, *Creation Untamed,* p. 15.

Jesus did not come to declare an eternal holiday for his followers. The year of Jubilee, which Jesus invoked in his teaching, did not mean a year of no work of any sort. It meant, rather, a newfound dedication to doing the Lord's work. Listen for a moment to how Jesus describes why he came to this earth in John 9:4: "I must work the works of the One who sent me while it is day; the night comes when no one can work." In this passage Jesus is not talking about the twenty-four-hour cycle of light and darkness, of work and rest, that we all experience all the time. No, he is looking at things from an eschatological perspective, and with some urgency. He believes he has a limited duration on this earth, and he also believes God has sent him on a mission to accomplish certain things in this life, and he knows that he needs to get on with what God sent him to do. In the same manner, we all have a limited duration on this earth to accomplish what God put us here for, and so we too should have some urgency about getting on with the job.

The portrait of Jesus in John 9:4 comports with the fact that God is constantly portrayed in the Bible as a vigorous worker in the world, not merely a creator but also a redeemer, and not merely a redeemer but also a sustainer, and in the last days also a quality control manager — that is, a judge of works (see, for example, Ps. 107; John 5:17). If, as Paul Minear stresses, the God of the Bible is "pre-eminently a worker,"[9] it is no surprise Jesus is as well — like Father, like Son. It is also no surprise, then, that once Jesus has gathered his Twelve he sends them out two by two on a work detail!

God the Worker and His Workmanship

In one sense we should have known this from the beginning. After all, isn't God depicted as working with his hands to fashion Adam

9. Minear, "Work and Vocation in Scripture," in *Work and Vocation: A Christian Discussion,* ed. J. Nelson (New York: Harper, 1954), p. 44.

in the first place from the dust of the earth (Gen. 2)? And aren't there various other places where God is depicted as a potter in the Bible, fashioning not just human beings, but all of creation? Psalm 8:3 says the universe is the work of his fingers! Picture a God so enormous that creating the vast universe is like fashioning small bits of clay. Or consider Job 38:14: "The earth takes shape like a lump of clay under a seal; its features stand out like those of a garment."

Furthermore, God doesn't set creation in motion and leave it to its own devices, like the watchmaker God envisioned by William Paley. No, God is hands-on, constantly tinkering and intervening, like a gardener always on the job, or a potter always at the wheel. Notice, for example, how Isaiah 45:7 and Amos 4:13, among other texts, reveal God designing particular features of our world, including ordering the seasons, sending the rain and sunshine (see also Ps. 74:17 and Jer. 31:35). God makes the animals (Gen. 1; Job 40–41), and above all he makes the human animal. This is why one of the enduring and endearing images of the relationship of God to his image is that found in Isaiah 64:8: "We are the clay, you are the potter; we are all the work of your hand." Indeed, Jeremiah even suggests that God shapes the unborn child in the womb (1:5).

Sometimes the image of God as potter and humans as his vessels is used to remind us, the vessels, that we are not in a position to question or critique our maker, who knows better than we what we were fashioned for. Certainly part of what the Bible says we are fashioned for is work, and worship, and rest, and play. "Shall what is formed say to him who formed it, 'He did not make me'? Can the pot say of the potter, 'He knows nothing'?" (Isa. 29:16; see also Isa. 45:9; Rom. 9:19-24). The image also suggests that, like a potter, God can refashion or shatter what he has made. God is hands-on, even after the initial creation of the vessel. But there is more. The image of potter and vessels suggests that different vessels are made for different purposes, and here we get into the realm of human vocation.

In a large house there are utensils not only of gold and silver but also of wood and clay, some for special use, some for ordinary. All who cleanse themselves of the things I have mentioned will become special utensils, dedicated and useful to the owner of the house, ready for every good work. (2 Tim. 2:20-21)

Notice three things about this passage from 2 Timothy: (1) different vessels are made for different purposes, but all have a purpose; (2) any vessel, if it cleanses itself, can be made useful for an honorable purpose; (3) the function of any and all such cleansed vessels is good works! Human beings were intended to work, and not just to do any kind of work, but to do good works, doing them in accord with the way we have been fashioned, the abilities we have been given, and therefore the vocations for which we are best suited.[10]

The potter is far from the only metaphorical description of God as a constant worker in the Bible. God is also described as metalworker, garment maker, dresser, gardener, farmer, winemaker, shepherd, tentmaker, builder, architect, musician, and composer.[11] What this vast array of images of God as worker suggests is that God is involved in every good aspect of life, and indeed is the inspirer and equipper of all good work. And what these images equally suggest is that God models good work, and indeed we become God's co-workers, as we shall discuss in due course. God not only models work of various kinds; he also shares creativity and power with those he works with, choosing to work in community, from the dawn of Creation when he says, "Let *us* make man . . ." and on an ongoing basis ever since. Fretheim concludes,

> While creatures are deeply dependent upon God for their creation and life, God has chosen to establish an *interdependent*

10. On all this see the discussion in R. Banks, *God the Worker: Journeys into the Mind, Heart, and Imagination of God* (Valley Forge: Judson, 1994), pp. 57-75.
11. For more on these, see Banks, *God the Worker*.

relationship with creatures with respect to both originating creation and continuing creation. God's approach to creation is communal, relational, and, in the wake of God's initiating activity, God works from within the world rather than on the world from without. . . . God's word in creation is often a communicating with others, rather than a top-down word. The creation texts thus show a sharp interest on God's part in sharing creative activity.[12]

While I would qualify this remark by saying that sometimes God does act on the creation from outside of the creation (e.g., in a theophany), basically Fretheim is right. Divine intervention, however, only supplements ongoing divine involvement within the space-time continuum.

I agree with Robert Banks when he says that we should not ignore or dismiss these metaphorical images as if they can tell us nothing of importance about God or ourselves:

Rather than leading us astray from a profound understanding of God, images such as those we have considered serve to draw us further into God's mind. They do so because they are themselves an expression of God's imagination. As such they give clearer definition of who God is and what God does. They also bring the everyday work in which we are engaged into closer contact with the character and purposes of God.[13]

These metaphors show us that God is indeed involved with, indeed revels in, the mundane and the ordinary. God is not just interested in our "religious" activities; he wants us to know the purpose and worth of all our work, and all of his work, whether it involves creation or re-creation, invention or redemption.

12. Fretheim, *Creation Untamed*, p. 18.
13. Banks, *God the Worker*, p. 283.

A Word to the Wise about Work's Purpose

I would suggest, without encouraging us to have Messiah complexes, that the same thing is true of each of us created in God's image that is true of God: we are called to be workers and that is an essential part of our purpose and mission on earth, all the more so since we now have God's salvation in Christ to proclaim to the world. We all have a limited time on earth, whether short or long, and we all have a God-given purpose on earth, regardless of whether we realize it.

Certainly one of the most miserable things a human can experience is the feeling of not knowing what she ought to be *doing* with her life. To avoid this feeling, we must grasp that our God-given purpose has a goal, a *telos,* to use the Greek term, not merely a terminus, and *it most certainly involves us working, indeed working hard, for the Kingdom.* We work with one eye on the horizon, realizing that the clock is ticking. But if we are working for the Kingdom, this means we also have a theological vision of work, a vision of what is worth doing and what is not, a desire to please the Master who gave us these tasks, and a teleological perspective striving for excellence — for anything worth doing is worth doing well, as well as is humanly possible. In short, our vision of work must be both eschatological and ethical, both theological and teleological.

On Being and Doing

We could debate endlessly whether being or doing is more important, but the fact is that both are equally important. We are to *be* new creatures in Christ, but as Paul says in Ephesians 2:13, we have been re-created in Christ "for good works," and not just to bask in the glow of our conversion experiences. One of my colleagues has a coffee cup that reads:

To be is to do — Plato
To do is to be — Aristotle
Do be do be do — Frank Sinatra

What this humorous mug shows is that being and doing are quite naturally intertwined and interdependent. This should be perfectly obvious to a Christian. You can't engage in Christian mission or work without first being a Christian! This should be obvious. But here is an important point — our purpose in life involves doing as much as being, and thus it is no wonder that if and when we come to the point of no longer having something meaningful and purposeful *to do,* something that takes us out of our own comfort zones and away from our pampering and serving ourselves, it is easy to see why we feel useless or purposeless in life. I am not suggesting that we can or should allow ourselves to be reduced to the equation *you are what you do;* I am simply saying that doing is essential to being if you are created in God's image, and there is no point in life when it ceases to be essential to who we are, short of death.

Bad Theologies of Work and Rest

I have been surprised over the years at what an ambivalent attitude many Christians display about work. I think some of this has to do with our theological assumptions. When we assume that salvation is purely a matter of being rescued by God, quite apart from our own best efforts, it is all too easy to develop a vision of work as something superfluous, as having nothing to do with our salvation. Too often we hear of a simplistic contrast between faith and works, or salvation and works, or grace and works, and too often this hard contrast leads to a distorted view of work.

My response to this is to say that while conversion is certainly a matter of salvation by grace through faith, that thereafter comes

Paul's challenge in Philippians 2:12-13, to "*work* out your salvation with fear and trembling, for it is God who *works* in you to will and to do." That is, salvation involves us *doing* something to work it out. Sanctification involves our own efforts, not just those of the Holy Spirit on our behalf and within us. Furthermore, any real definition of living faith affirms what James, the brother of Jesus, once told us — "faith without works is dead" (2:20). You can be as orthodox as the demons who confessed truly who Jesus was in the Synoptic Gospels, but if you are not *doing* the will of God, then you are not living out and living out of the faith that truly saves. Thus, *if even salvation involves works, good works of piety and charity, then even the most self-serving and self-centered Christian must admit that work is essential to not just the well-being, but the very being of a Christian throughout his or her life.*

The inherent connection between having a purpose in life and having some work to do is easily driven home if you take the time to visit a nursing home sometime. In these facilities (which are sometimes referred to as the antechamber of heaven), you will encounter senior citizens who fill out their days by playing checkers or board games, or eating, or watching mindless television shows, or, all too rarely, visiting with friends. If you ask them if anything is bothering them or if they need anything, one of the constant refrains you hear from so many of them is, "I just wish I had something useful or meaningful *to do.* I feel so useless here, like I've been thrown on the scrapheap of life." Indeed, and there is something profoundly wrong with a society that doesn't do what the Bible says should be done with those in their so-called golden years — that is, honor them, learn from them, and continue to allow them to do meaningful things for the Kingdom.

As it turns out, our American theology of retirement has no real biblical basis, and it leads to despair and longing and a sense of abandonment on the part of those who have been set off in a corner of society and told to hush and just "retire." On the one hand, senior citizens often feel like they are being punished when their families put them in a nursing or retirement home and wonder like schoolchildren what they have done to deserve it, what they have done wrong, why they are told they have nothing useful to contribute to society or life any more. And on the other end of the spectrum you have those early retirees who simply want to "live it up" and who brag on bumper stickers about spending their grandchildren's inheritance. Both these images of retirement are complete distortions of what the Bible says about sabbatical, rest, or the climax of a human life. And so one of the things we must do in this very study is not merely recover a biblical vision of work, but recover a biblical vision of its antonym, its silent partner as well — rest. So let us begin with a biblical, Kingdom definition of work.

Work Involves Calling

Work, from a biblical point of view, involves calling, vocation (not to be confused with vacation!), and, if done right, ministry. We often think of being "called" to be with a certain marriage partner, but in fact there are far more "call narratives" in the Bible in which God calls a person to *do* something than narratives about God calling a person to marry someone. The latter happens once in a while, but when it does it is often just plain disconcerting — think of the prophet Hosea being called to marry a prostitute! I doubt that at that moment Hosea was repeating the old cliché, "God has a wonderful plan for my life!"

Now, some theologians, notably Miroslav Volf, have objected to seeing work as a calling or associating calling with vocation.[14] Volf prefers to call work a "charism," something one is graced or gifted to do. I agree with what he is affirming here, but not with

14. See his otherwise very helpful book, *Work in the Spirit: Toward a Theology of Work* (Oxford: Oxford University Press, 1991).

what he is denying. Calling and work go together in the Kingdom, and this is perfectly apparent from Jesus' initial calling of the Twelve. What did he say, after all, but "Follow me, and I will make you fishers of human beings" (Mark 1:17)? Following is, of course, an activity, a doing of something, and more to the point, *being "fishers of human beings" is a job description.* Or take the example of Paul. His Damascus Road experience involved his being called to be the apostle to the Gentiles. This was his future vocation and work, and even his previous vocation of making tents would now be done in service to the larger task of evangelizing Gentiles and bringing them into the Kingdom. Calling, charism, gifting, vocation, ministry, and work are all interrelated things in the new order of God.

In fact, when it comes to vocation there is far more in the Bible about being called to serve, to save, to *do* something for God's cause than there is on any other subject. Whether it is God's calling of Abram to move and to become the father of many nations, or God's calling of Moses to liberate the Hebrew slaves in Egypt, or God's calling of Samuel to anoint David, all of these prophets, priests, judges, rulers, sages, servants, and the like are called to *do* certain, specific God-ordained tasks, just as Adam and Eve were in the garden. *Work is what weaves together the very fabric of a called person's identity, and fulfills it.*

Work, then, should be seen as one's vocation — what one is equipped and trained or gifted and experienced to do. Certain specific kinds of work are intended for a believer's life. Specific job descriptions or vocations may shift under God's direction, of course. Mark Twain once spoke to this very point:

Who was it who said, "Blessed is the man who has found his work"? Whoever it was he had the right idea in his mind. Mark you, he says his work — not somebody else's work. The work that is really a man's own work is play and not work at all. Cursed is the man who has found some other man's work and cannot lose it. When we talk about the great workers of the world we really mean the great players of the world. The fellows who groan and sweat under the weary load of toil that they bear never can hope to do anything great. How can they when their souls are in a ferment of revolt against the employment of their hands and brains? The product of slavery, intellectual or physical, can never be great.[15]

The Ends and Aims of Ethical Work

When done right, work is not merely purposeful but is also teleological — that is, it tends toward a certain goal or outcome. The right question to ask about work as a Christian is, Does this activity help or hinder the coming Kingdom? Does this activity promote the cause of Christ? Does this activity glorify God, and can it be offered up to God in thanksgiving? In short, can this work be doxological in character?[16]

Work, whether it involves plumbing a sink or plumbing the depths of the cosmos, in the hands of a Christian is ministry. The priesthood of all believers entails the ministry of all believers. We can thank Martin Luther for emphasizing this point and seeing its connection to the idea of work as a vocation. Work is an extension of Christ's ministry and the ministry he called his original disciples to do. This, of course, can involve a plethora of activities and professions.

Of course, as I have already suggested, there are limits to what can be considered legitimate, ethical work or ministry. Feeding human sheep is ministry; fleecing them is not. Ministering to prostitutes is legitimate; encouraging their profession is not. Helping people get out of debt by moral means is ministry; help-

---

15. "A Humorist's Confession," *New York Times*, November 26, 1905.
16. On which see Witherington, *We Have Seen His Glory.*

ing them make risky investments is not. Being a used car salesman can be a ministry; selling people things they do not need and that will not help them is not Christian work.

By now you will have caught the drift of this discussion. Before we engage in any sort of work, we have to ask whether it will glorify God and edify other persons, whether it can be an expression of love of God and love of neighbor. If the answer is no, we shouldn't be doing it.

Work is not a secular activity; it is a sacred one originally ordained by God, and so it must be undertaken in holy ways. And there is absolutely nothing wrong with good, old-fashioned honest labor or hard work, including manual labor. But whatever we do, we are to strive for excellence. The old saying goes that our Maker doesn't make any junk, and he likewise calls us to a high standard of excellence in what we produce. "Good enough" is not good enough when the standard of excellence is the example of Christ the worker.

Dirty Jobs Have Dignity

The wealthy Roman upper classes in Jesus' day had an aversion to dirty jobs, the kind that get your hands and clothes soiled. Not so ancient Jews like Jesus and Paul, who saw the dignity in manual labor of all sorts. Paul had no problem with being a tent maker or leather worker. Jesus had no problem with being a carpenter. Neither should we. Furthermore, none of our New Testament exemplars had a problem with mid-course corrections when it came to work, vocation, and ministry, whether temporary or permanent.

I used to live in northeast Ohio, where from time to time we would experience tornadoes. I remember on one occasion a twister hit near Hebron, an Amish haven that also had non-Amish residents. Once the twister had come and gone, the town's non-Amish residents were mostly to be found busily calling up FEMA and other agencies for help. The Amish, meanwhile, just set about rebuilding houses and barns without waiting for outside assistance. They even helped rebuild houses belonging to the non-Amish. They were good at carpentry and bricklaying and set right to work helping one and all in the community. They had a clear sense of Christian vocation — use your skills, your experience, your abilities, your vocation for the good of others, for the God who taught us to love our neighbors in practical ways.

I am well aware that most people in our world work just to live, just to stay alive. They have no choice. Work is a necessity, not a luxury, and often enough it is not even a choice. For most of the world's population, you just do what is there to be done and will put food on the table and clothes on the body. Barbara Brown Taylor thinks that sometimes it is a good exercise for those of us who live in the land of plenty to choose for a time to live differently, not least because it will give us a whole different perspective on and appreciation for work:

> Live as most people in the world live, preoccupied with survival. Wear the same clothes for a week because it is too cold to think about taking them off. Sleep as close to the fire as you can, welcoming the heat of another human body. Learn to shake your head at goals such as higher education, aerobic fitness, computer proficiency, and self-fulfillment. Long for the light you cannot procure for yourself, and feel your heart swell with gratitude — every single morning — when the sun comes up. Value warmth. Prize shelter. Praise the miracle of flowing water.[17]

Sometimes, by changing our work regimen, we get a better glimpse of what work is for, what work is like, what work is worth doing.

17. Taylor, *An Altar in the World*, p. 145.

On Work and the World

It is not a surprise that as the industrial age has gone forward we have lost our sense of connection between work and the world in which we work, between earthling and earth. Only a tiny minority of us are still farmers or gardeners. But we lose this sense of connection at our peril. We require air to breathe, water to drink, food to eat, shelter to live in, and work to do. All of this requires a living, breathing planet hospitable to human life in which to do such things. Jensen puts it this way:

> Work is always related to land, made possible because of resources of the land, and enables us to live from the bounty the land produces. No labor occurs apart from or removed from the land. Computer programming draws on minerals mined from the earth's crust; legal systems are attempts to live civilly on the land with one another. . . . And all . . . kinds of work are exchanged for food and resources reaped from the land. Good work draws us toward the land, reminds us of our indelible connection to earth, and teaches us to tread lightly.[18]

Literally everything we find on earth (except for meteorites), all our produce and all our products, has come directly or indirectly from the earth. We must never forget this fact. It is not just that we work on the earth or in the earth; it is that we work *with* the earth, and as our home and habitat we need to treat it with respect. We need an ecosphere in which to live, an environment in which the air is breathable and the water is potable. Too often we see nature, or the earth, as nothing more than a diversion or something to take a picture of, and we forget we are inextricably linked to the earth. Dust we are, and to dust we shall return.

18. D. Jensen, *Responsive Labor: A Theology of Work* (Louisville: Westminster John Knox, 2006), p. 113.

Christians who say, "This world is not our home; we're just passing through," have not taken stock of the theology of new creation at the end of the Bible, which reminds us that the finishing line for all of us is here on earth, not somewhere out there in a disembodied state in heaven. God, as it turns out, is an ecologist, and he intends to renew and redeem the earth, not just the earthlings; thus a part of our legitimate work on earth should be to foreshadow that renewal in the way we treat the earth, tend the garden, nurture the soil, clean the air, purify the waters, and "go green" in our use of renewable energy sources.

To say that the world is passing away, and so we can just throw it away, trash it, and move on somewhere else, like heaven, is neither tending the earth properly nor tilling the soil well. It is turning the world into a giant landfill, and the recent movie *WALL-E* gives us an idea of where this attitude leads.

Fortunately, the wastefulness and tragedy of this approach to living on the earth and off of the earth's bounty is beginning to dawn on some Christians. It has dawned on them that God is a conservationist, that this is his world, and that he wants us to take care of it. It is time for this kind of attitude to inform our vision of work. One implication, at least, is clear — there are some sorts of work that are unethical because they result in the destruction of the mother ship. For example, the form of mining called "strip mining" does far more harm than good, as a way of working the earth. "Destructive work pretends that we do not live from the earth and encourages roughshod ranging."[19] Of course, it is also true that it is wrong to take away work from a worker who needs it to support his family, without giving him some other meaningful work to do. There is an ethical obligation to the worker, as well as to the world itself.

19. Jensen, *Responsive Labor*, p. 113.

Of Labor and Labor-saving Devices

Take a minute to think about the phrase *labor-saving device.* What an odd concept it is. After all, it refers to a piece of equipment that has to be *used* to accomplish a task. That sounds to me like a labor-creating device! Of course, what is usually meant by the phrase is that if you labor with this device, it saves you having to do even harder, more backbreaking, more spine-bending labor. It takes the toilsomeness out of the toil . . . to some extent. It reverses the curse of the Fall, to some extent, and that is not a bad thing, especially if it allows us to do our work more efficiently, more completely, more perfectly.

We live in an age of artifice and the artificial — artificial light, artificial heat, artificial means of transportation. We are prisoners, captives of our gadgets. We are the computer and iPod culture. In such a culture, one loses sight all too easily of the real nature and character of work, good and godly work, and we desperately need a roadmap back to a place from which we might begin to understand work differently.

Barbara Brown Taylor argues,

> I live in a culture that regards physical labor as the lowest kind of labor. Gardening seems to be acceptable, along with washing the car and working out at the gym, but beyond that the general idea is to make enough money that you can pay other people to change your sheets, clean your toilets, mow your lawn, and raise your food. Typically, the people who do these things for a living are at the bottom of the economic ladder. If American culture admitted to caste, these laborers would be the shudras. Even those who do their own maintenance tend to collect labor-saving devices: dust-suckers, leaf-blowers, dishwashers, weed-eaters. Enormous people ride across their lawns equipped with cold beer holders. People with noise-reducing headphones on their heads strafe their driveways with hid-

eously loud machines, blowing leaves into the street that the first passing car will blow back into their yards again.[20]

And so it is that America has largely uncoupled itself not merely from the land and old-fashioned manual labor but also from any theological sense of the purpose, nature, necessity, and goals of work.

This uncoupling takes many forms. Once, when I was doing a program for a group of children, I asked them where food comes from. With one voice, they said, "The grocery store." This is not an unexpected answer; over the course of the twentieth century the demographics of the United States shifted from being over two-thirds rural to being 90 percent urban or suburban at the turn of the millennium. Food comes from the grocery store in the twenty-first century — of course it does. But the grocery store is not really its source, only its conveyer, and unless we know the source of things, we cannot know the sort of things they are and how our work is related to them.

The Uncoupling of the Earthling from the Earth

Why is it so important for us to have a sense of work, and its relationship to the earth? From a theological point of view it is in part because we are earthlings, or, as Genesis puts it, made from the dust of the earth, to which we will all one day return. Genesis tells us God created us to work this earth and to live in harmony with it. But with the Fall came a distortion in our vision of this work. We came to see it as burdensome.

We also forgot it all belongs to God. We forgot that in the final analysis there is no such thing as human or private property. "The earth is the Lord's and the fullness thereof" (Ps. 24:1). Not merely

20. Taylor, *An Altar in the World*, p. 146.

the tithe belongs to God — it all does. We are stewards of God's property, and this must necessarily change entirely our view of work.[21] We are God's servants, God's employees, God's workers. We brought no "stuff" into the world with us, nor can we take any of it with us when we die. Our theology of work must be related to our theology of property, and vice versa. Lots of people talk about their "life work." It is right that those two words should be intertwined. There would be no life without work, and no work without life.

Our goal in this opening chapter has been to expose ourselves to the *kinds* of theological and ethical considerations that lead to a proper perspective on work as calling, vocation, ministry. The truth is that even when work seems like drudgery, if it is done to God's glory it is good in character, and if it is done for the edification of others it is at the very least divine drudgery, not mere toil, not mere activity. It has meaning, purpose, direction. It is Kingdom-bringing.

So, what will be your magnum opus — your great and magnificent work done in the light of the day and in the shadow of the Almighty? Whatever it is, you need to get on with it, because the Kingdom is coming, indeed, "the night is coming when no one can work" (John 9:4). And when it comes, there will be no night shift, only a graveyard shift. So let's roll up our sleeves, wash our hands, and get busy with understanding work in light of the Word and in service to the world. Perhaps we will come to understand what it means to "labor not in vain" (1 Cor. 15:58) for the sake of the Kingdom and its King.

---

21. On this see my little book entitled *Jesus and Money: A Guide for Times of Financial Crisis* (Grand Rapids: Brazos, 2010).

CHAPTER TWO

A Theology of Work as Vocation

The doctrine of vocation amounts to a comprehensive doctrine of the Christian life, having to do with faith and sanctification, grace and good works. It is a key to Christian ethics. It shows how Christians can influence culture. It transfigures ordinary, everyday life with the presence of God. . . . The priesthood of all believers did not make everyone into church workers; rather it turned every kind of work into a sacred calling.

Gene E. Veith[1]

Accent on the Individual?

Western culture since the Reformation has put an ever-increasing emphasis on the individual; in fact, several components of the Reformation accelerated tendencies already extant in this direction. First, there was the leveling idea of the priesthood of all believers, which was closely tied to the second notion of the sacred calling or vocation of all believers to various sorts of godly work:

1. *God at Work: Your Christian Vocation in All of Life* (Wheaton: Crossway, 2002), pp. 17, 19.

[The] doctrine of vocation encourages attention to each individual's uniqueness, talents, and personality. These are valued as gifts from God, who creates and equips each person in a different way for the calling He has in mind for that person's life. The doctrine of vocation undermines conformity, recognizes the unique value of every person, and celebrates human differences; but it sets these individuals into a community with other individuals, avoiding the privatizing self-centered narcissism of secular individualism.[2]

So argues Gene Veith with some confidence. I am less confident than he is that Protestantism in its accent on the individual has countered more than contributed to modern individualism. In any case, with that individualism has come equally modern notions about work and pay and private property, as well as, of course, the Puritan work ethic, which we looked at earlier. Not all these things are unqualified goods, particularly in view of how they have often made it difficult to maintain the unity of the body of Christ.

Furthermore, in the process of individualization we lost contact with the biblical notion of collective personality — that is, how we get our true identity through the group we belong to, in this case, the body of Christ. Most of my students are stunned when they read Philippians 2:12 in the Greek and discover that "work out your salvation with fear and trembling, for it is God who works in you to will and to do" is an exhortation to a group, and the word "you" in this passage is in the plural! Salvation, in these terms, is a group project. And so is work. While we can rightly commend the Reformation notion that all Christians, not just ordained clergy, have callings or vocations, that does not justify the excessive individualism that has come to characterize much of American Protestantism. But when we talk about a Ref-

2. Veith, *God at Work*, p. 21.

ormation theology of the vocation of all Christians, it is well to talk about the person who put this ball into play in the first place — Martin Luther.

Luther, Providence, and the Two Kingdoms

Behind the Reformation theology of work as vocation stands Luther's view of the providence of God, namely that God works through means human and natural to accomplish his will. We can see this especially plainly through a Lutheran exegesis of Romans 13, which points out not only that all authority is from God, including the authority of the Emperor, but that governmental authorities are God's agents or instruments to execute justice. The way Luther reconciled the last portion of Romans 12, which speaks of reconciliation and forgiveness, with the beginning of Romans 13 was by means of the doctrine of vocation. That is, what is appropriate in one vocation is not appropriate in another.

It was appropriate, Luther believed, for the governing official to punish the thief or the murderer, but not appropriate for Christians who are not governing officials to do so. Different vocations involve different roles. The problem, of course, with this approach to the matter is that if perchance a Christian were to become a governing official — what then? Should such a Christian put his allegiance to the Sermon on the Mount on hold for the duration of his employment and execute justice as God's agent of wrath? Or should he act on the basis of his civic vocation in one venue and act another way at home, when he is off the job? Or should he have abstained from undertaking the vocation of being a judge — or, say, a policeman — in the first place? The theology of spheres, kingdoms, and multiple vocations can lead to a certain schizophrenia in the Christian life about when we should or should not obey the teaching of Jesus in the Sermon on the Mount. Nothing in the sermon itself suggests that Jesus was saying that obedience to such teachings should be limited to the private sector, or when we are "off duty" from some civic profession.

Gene Veith explains the dichotomy this way when it comes to how Christians should approach a crime committed against them:

> When someone breaks into our car and steals our stereo, we are not to hunt down the culprit and shoot him dead. We do not have the authority. We do not have the vocation to do that. Rather we are supposed to call the police. They do have the authority and the vocation to bring criminals to justice, and judges and jailers have the vocation to punish them.[3]

But saying, "That's not my job," does not absolve the disciple of the responsibility to *always* obey the teachings of the Lord. The Lutheran approach to the matter relies on the notion of God as *Deus absconditus,* the God who is hidden in everyday life, hidden in human vocations and always at work. And behind that notion is, of course, the Augustinian idea that God has predestined all things that ever come to pass, either actively by *causing* them to happen, or passively by *allowing* them to happen (but even the things "allowed" by God are just as certain to happen, even if they are not in apparent accord with God's revealed will).

However, it is one thing to say, "God uses civil magistrates to protect us. He uses fathers to care for us, and spouses to bless us. . . . God is working even through those who do not know Him."[4] It is entirely another to say, "God used the Nazis to punish Jews who refused to accept Christ as their savior" — and indeed some Lutherans did say such awful things before and during World War II. The problem with Augustinianism is that it makes God the ultimate author of sin and evil, if all human beings, re-

3. Veith, *God at Work,* p. 33.
4. Veith, *God at Work,* p. 33.

gardless of their behavior, are God's agents and all actions ultimately go back to God.

Luther's theology does not leave room for a "contrary secondary cause" in any meaningful sense. And even without an extensive theological discussion, we can see that there are problems with Luther's approach to the theology of vocation. To take an extreme example, is pimping really a vocation through which God works for good, and are pimps the agents of God? If the answer to this is no, then it follows that there are some vocations, tasks, callings that are not of God, some which God wants nothing to do with, some with which God is not secretly cooperating. Of course it is true that God can "work all things together for good for those who love God, who are called according to his purpose" (Rom. 8:28), but frankly that has nothing to do with God destining some to be wicked, some to be pimps, some to be murderers, and so on.

Vocation Comes from Calling

Further complicating Luther's view is the fact that, in the Bible, a vocation that comes from God comes with a calling that comes from God. The fishermen who heard Jesus call them responded, and they were made fishers of human beings. Here the link between responding to a call from God and taking up a vocation from God is clear. It is so clear, in fact, that in the early Middle Ages some Christian theologians made the mistake of associating vocation *only* with those who were called to be a monk or a nun, a priest or a bishop. The distinction was made between sacred callings and everything else. This, however, is as big a mistake as calling all professions vocations.

Part of the problem by the time we get to the Reformation is that Luther held to what we could call a "two-kingdoms" model of analyzing reality — that there was a secular kingdom and a sacred kingdom and different rules and even different vocations applicable to each. This distinction, however, unwittingly furthered the notion of a split, a hard distinction, between the sacred and the secular. But the Bible says nothing about God having two kingdoms, one spiritual and one physical, one sacred and one secular. The only Kingdom in the Bible that has the name God appended to it is the one Jesus claimed to be bringing in through his preaching, teaching, healing, and dying and rising. All other kingdoms are called by Jesus the kingdoms of this world. This doesn't mean God has nothing to do with such earthly kingdoms — indeed, God authorizes and empowers them. But it does mean that we are mistaken if we say that *God* has two kingdoms and operates on different principles in each.

God at Work, or We Work with God, or Both?

But what about a passage like Ephesians 2:10? "We are God's workmanship, created in Christ Jesus for good works, which God prepared beforehand, that we should walk in them." Those in the Lutheran tradition would say that "we are God's workmanship" means not merely that God has fashioned us and empowered us for good works, but rather that "God is at work in us to do the work he intends."[5] Yet I would argue that Paul is using the language of agency here, and is talking about a viable secondary cause.

That is, God has authorized, empowered, and purposed us to do good works, but it is *we* who are either doing them or not, as God's representatives. We should not simply assume that God "does" everything in the universe, merely using us as his pawns, his puppets, or even his instruments. We human beings are not pieces on a chess board; we are persons created in the image of God, and God relates to us by and large as personal agents, which

5. Veith, *God at Work*, p. 38.

involves, among other things, giving us space to act on our own, empowered by the Almighty.

I would suggest this is precisely why Paul speaks in 1 Corinthians 3 of our being co-laborers with God. Our work can be distinguished from God's. The one is not simply the other. The two should not be fused or confused. In the biblical view, working in tandem with another person involves *koinonia*, a sharing in common or a participation in common. It does not involve, at least not regularly, a co-opting of one party by the other, or one party merely being used by the other to achieve his ends. And so it is when we work with God. It is good to note at this juncture, as Miroslav Volf does, that there is widespread agreement between most Protestant and Catholic theologians that the Bible affirms a view of human work as "co-operation with God."[6] It is evident as early as Genesis 2, when the absence of vegetation on the new earth is given both a divine and a human cause: God has not yet sent rain, and no human being has yet tilled the ground. "There is a mutual dependence between God and human beings in the task of preservation of creation."[7]

Distinguishing Faith and Works Too Radically

The Lutheran view also establishes an unhelpful dichotomy between faith, which ostensibly serves God, and works, which ostensibly serve our neighbor. The apostle James, who wrote that faith without works is dead, would hardly have agreed with such a distinction. Surely, when we are created in Christ for good works, those works are done on behalf of and for the glory of God and *also* for the help of our neighbors. The separation of service to

6. See his *Work in the Spirit: Toward a Theology of Work* (Eugene: Wipf and Stock, 2001), p. 98.

7. Volf, *Work in the Spirit*, p. 99.

God and to neighbor works no better than the separation of the two kingdoms.

Luther was so insistent on this division of labor that he came to excoriate monks who believed that, by praying and saying the Mass, they were doing good works and serving God. In his view, in the spiritual kingdom God serves human beings, not the other way around. Hence the distinction maintained by Veith: "In vocation, we are not doing good works for God — we are doing good works for our neighbor."[8] And thus our vocations are said to have nothing to do with the process of working out our salvation with fear and trembling, nothing to do with our ongoing sanctification. What Lutherans are trying to guard against, of course, is the idea of salvation by works or good deeds. But is this really a biblically defensible position? It is certainly not Paul's view. Look, for example, at 1 Thessalonians 4:3: "This is God's will, your sanctification, that you should avoid sexual immorality." This may seem to have little to do with our topic of work, but it shows in no uncertain terms that what we *do* as Christian believers does indeed affect our sanctification, our ongoing salvation (and in the case of sexual immorality affects it negatively). This examination of Luther's theology makes it clear that our theology of work and vocation will be affected, if not entirely determined, by our theology of how God works in the world and our theology of salvation as well.

Service to Neighbor Is Service to Christ

It is part of our vocation to love and serve one another. In essence, every job, if done to the right ends and for the right purposes, is part of the "service industry." It should be clear, however, that we are not just serving our neighbor when we feed the hungry, clothe the naked, and visit the imprisoned. As Matthew 25:35-40 makes

8. Veith, *God at Work*, p. 39.

evident, we are also serving God when we do such things. It is a mistake to distinguish too radically our service to Christ and our service to neighbor. This is not because Christ is somehow "hidden" in our neighbor. It is because Jesus wants us to treat others as we would treat him *if he were here in the flesh.* This is the language of agency and hospitality and identifying with the other. It is not about Christ's being "hidden" in the neighbor. Nor is it that I "see Christ" in the destitute neighbor. It is that in encountering this neighbor I see an opportunity to serve her as Christ would do. In such a transaction, the one following the pattern of Christ is the *server,* not the one being served, for Christ was a self-sacrificial server (see Mark 10:45). W.W.J.D. should be our mantra: *What would Jesus do?*

One of the valuable insights of Veith's treatment of work and vocation is the idea that work is not simply what one does for pay in the workplace. One's vocation and work can be to take care of young children at home, it can be to volunteer at the blood center, it can be to work pro-bono at the legal aid society, and so on. Viable, valuable work, and the vocation and calling to do it, is not limited to work done for hire. Of course in our world, and particularly in the United States, too many people are made to feel useless because they are apparently not "gainfully employed" or even are just "underemployed." But it is a huge mistake to evaluate the merits or worth of one's work on the basis of whether one is remunerated for it, much less on the basis of *how much* one is remunerated for it.

The Calling and Leading of God, and the Choices of Others

Another valuable point that Veith makes is that our vocation is hardly entirely in our own hands. This is one reason it is called a "calling." We do not simply choose our vocations. We are led to them, and this implies that we must be open to hearing from God what he is calling us to do in life. Even when we have been called and gifted to do something, God does not simply leave us to our own devices. Rather, he guides us and steers us in our work. This does not mean, of course, that the role or job we find ourselves in when we become Christians suddenly becomes our vocation. Of course not. When God calls a thief, his stealing does not become a vocation. Rather, God calls him to leave his thievery behind. The same may be true of any of us, in any occupation.

Volf is right that there is a dangerous ambiguity in Luther's distinction between a person's inner spiritual call and the external calling which comes through her "station in life." How do we reconcile these two callings — particularly if the external one is incompatible with repenting and responding to the gospel? Too close an integration of calling and vocation is part of the problem, but the other part of the problem is the assumption that whatever is, has been destined by God.[9]

Luther's understanding of "staying in one's station in life and seeing it as one's calling and/or vocation from God" of course also flies in the face of the evidence of the Gospels, where Jesus calls disciples *away* from their nets, *away* from tax collecting, and, in Jesus' own case, away from carpentry. The language of calling must be distinguishable from the language of vocation (and gifting), not least because all Christians are called out of darkness to love God and neighbor and fulfill the Great Commission, and the *calling* itself does not specify a vocation other than this general one of fulfilling the Great Commandment and the Great Commission. When Paul in Romans 12 or 1 Corinthians 12 wants to talk about tasks, he refers to the way the Spirit has gifted different called persons differently. Vocations differ, but the calling of God is to all those converted.

Most of us at some point in our Christian lives have had the experience of feeling "led" to do something, and that something

9. See Volf, *Work in the Spirit*, pp. 107-8.

often involves a change of vocation. David, for example, was minding his own business being a shepherd when a prophet came and anointed him heir apparent to the throne. This sort of divine intervention, providence, serendipity happens. It happened to me some fifteen years ago. I was minding my own business teaching at a seminary in northeast Ohio when I received a phone call asking if I would consider coming and teaching at Asbury Seminary. After wrestling with this for a while, and consulting the Lord, my wife, and others, I took the job. Vocation, and even change of venue for the same kind of vocation, is not purely in the hands of the individual in question. It is the result of God's calling one to do something, God's leading, but it can be distinguished from the call itself.

Christians know that they are called *to* their vocations, not in or by their vocations.[10] Of course, sometimes Christians practice call forwarding, like Moses in Exodus 3, trying to pass God's call to him along to his brother Aaron. Or sometimes we are not merely underemployed but wrongly employed, and it is no surprise that when this is true God tends to make us profoundly uneasy, unsettled, and unsatisfied with what we are doing, even when on a certain level we would very much like to keep doing it. He sends us an internal memo that we should not be comfortable with what we are doing. And of course sometimes Christians flat-out reject God's call on their life and go off and do something else. It is good, however, to remind ourselves that life is not just about the choices we make. It's often about choices others make for us or about us.

As much as we like to think that we live in a world of choices and that the lives we live are determined by the choices we make, Christians in fact know that life is as much about what has happened to us as about making choices. I did not choose to be born into the Witherington family, or to be born in the United States, or to be born in North Carolina, or to have a baby sister. I did not

10. Veith, *God at Work*, p. 50.

choose to go to Northwood Elementary School, and so on. I did not choose to have brown eyes and hair and to stop growing when I reached about 5′10″. You catch my drift. The question is this: Are calling and vocation things we have a choice about, like where we attend college or whom we marry, or things that are determined for us, like who our parents are?

I would guess that most of us grew up assuming that we had some choice about what we would "become." The perennial question asked of young people, "What do you want to be when you grow up?" implies that their own personal desires and aspirations have something to do with it. Of course, more factors are involved beyond simple desire, including our gifts, graces, aptitudes, learning styles, and the like, and clearly we do not choose to be gifted, or not gifted, in particular areas or fields.

I started my freshman year of college on a pre-med track. But after my first few classes in organic chemistry and calculus and the like, it became clear that I was not really cut out for a career in medicine, because I could not make the grades necessary to get into a good medical school. God had not wired my brain that way, regardless of how much I studied and how hard I tried. "Finding your vocation, then, has to do, in part, with finding your God-given talents (what you can do) and your God-given personality (what fits the person you are)."[11]

Most of us, sadly, have studied under a teacher or two who had all the mental aptitude in the world for understanding their subject matter, but who couldn't teach their way out of a paper bag. I had such a calculus teacher in college, and the running joke was that the difference between this teacher and the textbook was that the book did not stutter. This joke was rather cruel, but an inability to go beyond a textbook in making subject matter accessible or interesting to students is a good sign that a person is probably not called to be a teacher.

11. Veith, *God at Work*, pp. 52-53.

Our personalities and interpersonal skills are part of what should determine what work we do. And it is a mistake to assume that our calling will necessarily cut against the grain of our natural inclinations and instincts and desires. This is by no means always true. There is a sense in which each person is a unique combination of talents and gifting and personality and education and training, all of which factor into what sort of calling or vocation we should pursue. One thing is clear: when we find our calling, we are unlikely to find it boring, though it may be onerous in various ways. It is also unlikely that we will hate what we are called to do, though there may be days or even longer periods when difficulties or even dangers make us wish very strongly that we were called to something else.

The writer of Proverbs reminds us that "the human mind plans the way, but the LORD establishes the steps" (16:9). There is a synergistic relationship between believers and the Lord when it comes to good and godly plans and their execution. God makes a way, paves the way, for us to do what we ought to do, but at the same time our free, un-predetermined choices are woven into the divine design. There is a mystery to this, and it is just as wrong to suggest "it's all God's doing," as it is to suggest "it's all my doing." We must work out what God works into our lives, and this includes our vocations. We plan, and pray, and strive, and work, but we must leave the results in God's hands, because no human being can control the outcome of all his efforts.

The old road construction signs used to say, "Men working." But in any calling worthy of the name, it is never merely human beings working; it is also God working. The sooner we swallow our humility pills and see ourselves as lowly junior partners and co-laborers with God, rather than the only laborers on the scene, the sooner we will have a real grasp of work, vocation, and calling. But here is the exciting news. While doubtless God could have done it all by himself, instead he has chosen to involve us in his work! As Paul puts it, we are stewards of the mysteries of God, we are co-laborers in the vineyard, we are ministers of the grace of God, and we are neighbors shedding the love of God abroad to the world.

I agree with Veith that our calling comes from outside ourselves. It is not something we discover exclusively through introspection or self-analysis. If even a prophet like Elijah had to go somewhere where he could hear again the voice of God calling him in the midst of the cacophony of the world, why should it be any different for us?

Veith also points out that when a person is hired — whether to a law firm, a medical practice, a university, or elsewhere — not only is it not merely a choice of the individual. It is also not merely a simple choice of the employer. In virtually all cases there is a complex hiring process involving many different individuals, committees, and so on, working interdependently to discern whether any given candidate will be able to fill her vocation with that particular institution. Only when a person is completely self-employed is this process eliminated, and even then we could say that a self-employed person's clients are necessary contributors to the process of discerning her vocation.

Charism or Vocation?

The theologian Miroslav Volf would like to change the terms of the discussion from "vocation" to "charism" when it comes to our work.[12] I disagree, and here it will be helpful to explain why. In the first place, the term "charism" as found in 1 Corinthians 7 refers to the grace gift either to remain single for the Lord or to remain married in the Lord. It has nothing directly to do with our vocation. Second, in 1 Corinthians 12 and Ephesians 4, differing persons are said to "be" gifts to the church ("God has given some to

12. See Volf, *Work in the Spirit*, pp. 111-19.

be apostles . . ."), but the gift or charism here is the person, not the work! I am not denying that this or that person has been gifted to do some specific work, for no doubt he has been called and gifted to do so. But the work itself is not called a gift; the ability to do the work is.

The problem is that Volf defines the term "gift" wrongly, and in some respects too broadly.[13] I agree that the Spirit gives gifts to everyone, and these gifts equip people for various forms of service, ministry, and work. But the gifts are not the work or vocation. Volf is right that we should not limit the discussion to specifically religious work or work directly involving sharing the gospel when we are talking about what the Spirit equips individuals to do (see, e.g., Exod. 35:2-3). All sorts of tasks are undertaken in the Bible under the aegis and by the empowerment of the Spirit (see Judg. 3:10; 1 Sam. 16:13; 23:2; Prov. 16:10). The Christian knows, however, that the Spirit is the one who decides who gets what gift (1 Cor. 12:11).

Volf is absolutely right, though, that the Spirit not merely humanizes but Christianizes work — the Spirit doesn't lead anyone to do something dishonest, dishonorable, destructive, unloving, and so on. And since the Spirit is the Spirit of Jesus Christ, the Spirit enables persons to imitate the behavior of Christ in what they do, including in their work. This automatically eliminates certain jobs for Christians. "The significance and meaning of Christians' work lie in their cooperation with God in the anticipation of the eschatological *transformatio mundi* [transformation of the world]."[14] The Spirit both enables our work and provides guidance and guidelines about what work we should do.

---

13. For example, he even wants to suggest that non-Christians have a "charism" from the Spirit to do their good work (p. 118). Without denying that the Spirit works outside the body of Christ, I would assert that Paul's theology of spiritual gifts cannot so readily be extended to non-Christians as Volf's thesis suggests.

14. Volf, *Work in the Spirit*, p. 117.

Theocentric or Ecclesiocentric Views of Calling?

Here I have to disagree strongly with Gene Veith. He has this to say about the relationship between calling and the institutions or organizations that employ us: "In the church, pastors are called by congregations, that is, their divine call comes to them through the workings of the church as a whole, which selects them, trains them, and ordains them into ministry. A woman who 'feels called to ministry' . . . cannot be called to a church that does not call her."[15] There are at least three problems with this whole line of reasoning.

First, calls come from God, not from particular churches or groups of church leaders. The church may help a person discern her calling, may help nurture her in her calling, but the church is not the "caller" of this person. This is perfectly clear from New Testament examples ranging from Peter to Paul to Apollos to various others. The call comes directly from God in Christ, whether it is on a Damascus road, or sitting on a beach by a fire, or somewhere else. The church is not Christ, and it does not do the calling. The body is not the Head. The job of the body is to recognize when someone has been called and then to affirm that calling by helping put the person to work.

Second, a person is frequently called to serve a church that has not called him. Think back to Elijah's experience in the wilderness in 1 Kings 18. In effect he says to God, "The Israelites have rejected me and are about to lynch me. Clearly I am not called to serve them." What was God's response to this line of thinking? It was not to agree with the discouraged Elijah, but rather to say, "Go back to your tasks which I have assigned you, knowing I will give you some more help."

Third, even on a practical basis, most Christian denominations have an appointive process, and frequently ministers are

15. Veith, *God at Work*, pp. 56-57.

sent to local churches that did not call them, did not specifically ask for them, but accepted them as a reasonable appointment by a bishop or district superintendent. Of course there is a process of discernment, and individual churches are allowed to be consulted about their perception of their needs, but at the end of the day ministers are not, and should not be, called or appointed by local congregations. Giving such power to local churches is a clear violation of New Testament polity regarding elders, deacons, teachers, and other leaders as it is articulated in the Pastoral Epistles and elsewhere. While some Christian denominations have departed from it, the New Testament does suggest a hierarchical ecclesial system for appointing ministers, though we may well want to debate the particulars.[16] In the end, then, we cannot look to Veith's portrayal of the calling of ministers as a model for the calling of Christians to their vocations.

What Counts as a Calling?

Is marriage a calling or vocation? I do not think so. Marriage requires a grace gift, but it is not a job, it is not a form of employment, it is not a task. Paul speaks to this very issue in 1 Corinthians 7. He says that some have the *charism* to be single for the sake of the Lord, and some to be married in the Lord, but each Christian must discern what state or station he is gifted to be in. Both marriage and celibacy require a certain grace gift. Yet just because something requires grace does not make it a vocation, or a calling, or a job, or a task. Paul believes that whatever one's social status in life, one can be a Christian in that situation and status (1 Cor. 7:17-24).

The real proof that Paul is not thinking here of marriage or celibacy as a vocation comes when he says in the same context that

16. See my discussion in *Letters and Homilies for Hellenized Christians,* vol. 1 (Downers Grove: InterVarsity, 2007), on the Pastoral Epistles.

slaves need not change their status in order to be true Christians, but that if they have the opportunity to change their situation or their social status they should avail themselves of it. Paul evidently does not believe that being a slave is a good or godly vocation, a view that becomes especially clear in the Epistle to Philemon. Once one is a brother, one should no longer have to be a slave. In short, the discussion in 1 Corinthians 7 is not about vocation, but rather is about social relationships and situations and social status, a very different matter.

Gene Veith, following the Lutheran tradition, is also prepared to say that "the family is the most basic of all vocations."[17] I have to disagree with this on several levels. Above all, one is simply born (or adopted) into a family, as we have discussed above. Family *happens,* but it is not a calling or vocation. It is a grace gift.

What about roles within the family? Can they be vocations? I think it would be possible to make a case for seeing a person's main task or vocation at various times of life, or even of the week, as being a father or mother; these are tasks a person takes up freely if he or she gets married and then chooses to have children. And God can indeed call someone to have as his or her main vocation being a father or mother for a season of life. But I would want to distinguish between an individual's main task, by which I mean the one which takes up most of one's time, and the Christian's primary tasks, that is, those involving the Great Commandment and the Great Commission. Here is where our discussion about an eschatological perspective on earthly relationships must come into play.

First, marriage is an earthly institution for our earthly good. It is not an eternal reality, as texts such as Romans 7 or 1 Corinthians 7 make perfectly clear. Second, it is equally clear that Jesus *did* call the disciples away from their families to more important tasks at various points in time. Indeed, Peter complains about this at

17. Veith, *God at Work*, p. 78.

one juncture and asks about the rewards in the Kingdom he will get for the sacrifice he has made (Mark 10:28-31). And Paul says that, in light of the eschatological situation, the husband and wife must recognize the earthly contingency of their relationship and live "as if not," to use his exact words.

Under these circumstances, it must be said that the call to make disciples of other human beings can indeed at times supersede the call to simply be a good parent or spouse. As the early Jews said, while bringing someone into this world is a good deed, bringing them into the world to come is a better one, and indeed in various ways a more important one. What good is it if a person lives a long, healthy life and gains the whole world, and loses his soul? In the end, such good comes to an end. The Great Commission does not say, "Go get everyone married in all the nations," but rather, "Go make disciples of all the nations." There is a danger of turning the family into an idol, when its priorities are allowed to supersede those of the Kingdom.

Not All Tasks Are Vocations, Not All Gainful Employment Is a Calling

Even necessary tasks in life are not always or necessarily vocations. For example, every human being needs to take time to eat. This is most certainly a task, and even a good one, but it should never be seen as one's vocation! Not everything we do, nor even every good and necessary thing we do, should be seen as a calling, a vocation, a person's work.

This extends, as I have already suggested, to various forms of being gainfully employed. For example, a drug dealer or a prostitute may well work hard and make a good deal of money, but these "jobs" are not vocations or callings given by God. Veith suggests applying the test: Can this job be an expression of love of neighbor (and, I would add, love of God)? If the answer is no, then it cannot be one's vocation or calling in life. It may be work, it may even be hard work, but if it harms the neighbor and ruins people's relationships with God, family, others, not to mention themselves, then it is hardly something God would have us do.

How Christians Should Work

More helpful is Veith's discussion of *how* we should take up our tasks, our vocations in life, what sort of workers we should be. He writes,

> There is no distinctively Christian way of being a carpenter, or an actor or a musician. Christian and non-Christian factory workers, farmers, lawyers, and bankers do pretty much the same thing. Perhaps a Christian might be unusually honest or ethical, but honesty and ethical behavior is expected of the non-Christian worker as well. Remember that non-Christians too have been placed in their positions and are being used by the God they do not even know.[18]

The reason, however, that there is no particularly Christian way to do things right is because "rightness" and "truth" have been ingrained into the very fabric of reality, including human reality. All human beings are created in the image of God, and therefore all human beings know something about right and wrong (see Rom. 1–2), and therefore they know something about what honesty and integrity are about. Of course, in a fallen world not everyone is particularly concerned about honesty and integrity, and so if a Christian does his job especially well, striving for excellence,

18. Veith, *God at Work*, p. 68. While there is truth to this, I would hesitate to say that non-Christian persons have a vocation in the Christian sense, because they have not responded to a call from God to do what they do, or at least usually not.

working hard, and being a person of integrity and honesty, he may well stand out from the run-of-the-mill worker who is not motivated by a love of God and neighbor and a striving to please both.

But pleasing God is one thing in our work, impressing God quite another. Veith puts it this way:

> Wealth, possessions, position, and all marks of prestige mean less than nothing to God, who delights to exalt the humble and send the rich away empty (Luke 1:52-53). . . . It is important to remember in understanding vocation that He does not operate as the world does, that He may call us to what the world and we ourselves might consider a position that is "beneath us," lacking the glamour and importance that we would like for ourselves.[19]

Christians are called by the Scriptures to be busy, not busybodies. This is why Paul says to the Thessalonians, "aspire to live quietly, to mind your own affairs, and to work with your hands, as we instructed you, so that you may live properly before outsiders and be dependent on no one" (1 Thess. 4:11-12). The Christian perspective on work is that it does not involve meddling, but rather getting on with doing our own tasks. As both this text and Galatians 6 suggest, one of the proximate goals of work is to enable us to support ourselves and our families. Christians are not called to be dependent on their family or friends — or on the government. We are called to make our contribution to society, not least by not unnecessarily draining that society's emergency resources when we could be out supporting ourselves. Of course there are times when we may find ourselves out of work or unable to work because of injury, illness, and so forth. But so long as we are able, we are to carry our own weight, bear our own load in life. Notice that in the passage above,

19. Veith, *God at Work*, pp. 70-71.

Paul specifically mentions that outsiders are watching. There is an element of witness in how we live our lives, including how we do our jobs and pursue our vocations.

Ethics and Vocation

A code of ethics governs every good profession. Physicians are guided by the Hippocratic Oath, which mandates that they foster healing and life. A doctor who performs abortions therefore stands in violation of this oath. Plumbers may not have a specific oath they are sworn to uphold, but they must still work ethically. They cannot, for instance, install parts they know to be of poor quality, or mislead their customers into thinking small problems are larger than they really are, in order to charge more. When we see such professions as Christian callings, then in addition we have to ask a further question: "If I do this, this way, am I fulfilling the commandment to love my neighbor?"

Veith is also right that certain activities are only ethical, and even legal, within certain professions. For example, a surgeon has a right to cut me open, and if she does, she may well be saving my life.[20] On the other hand, virtually no one else has the right to cut me open — not even a doctor trained in another field of medicine. Likewise, only a judge has the authority to sentence someone to prison, and only a teacher has the authority to pass or fail a student. Put another way, it is the office that has the power and authority; the office holder has no such personal right, power, or authority.[21] We sometimes talk in our society about "taking the law into our own hands," but what we actually are doing is taking the lawmaker or law enforcer's vocation into our own hands, which is not only illegal but immoral.

20. Veith, *God at Work,* p. 137.
21. Veith, *God at Work,* p. 138.

Of course, Christians will legitimately disagree about whether some tasks can be considered Christian callings. Take, for example, the profession of being a soldier. Many Christians throughout the years have believed that being a soldier is, or can be, a legitimate Christian vocation; but in my judgment, while a Christian can be a chaplain to soldiers or a medic, he cannot actually be a soldier, precisely because doing so amounts to putting his vocation above his obligation to obey the dictates of Christ, who called us to love our enemies, pray for those who persecute us, do no harm, and indeed turn the other cheek rather than return violence for violence. Killing is always a violation of loving one's neighbor as oneself. Again, I know many Christians do not hold this view, but I am comforted by the fact that many of the Church Fathers who reflected on this very subject agree with me. Tertullian, for instance, in explaining Matthew 26:52 writes that the Lord unbelted Peter and thereby "unbelted every soldier." Thus, he concludes, a Christian may not make war nor "serve even in peace" ("On Idolatry," XIX). If there is a hierarchy of ethical values, then explicitly Christian values have to trump society's values for the individual Christian when they conflict. Furthermore, any profession that inherently entails sinning and violating the law of Christ is not a profession a Christian should engage in. I do not think a Christian should be a soldier; nor do I think a Christian should, for instance, work in the casino business or the tobacco industry.

Veith uses the notion of vocation to think about what tasks a Christian should actually attempt, and I agree this is helpful. For example, take the person who attempts to fix his own electrical wiring when he has no aptitude, training, or skill at such a task. The results can be shocking! Veith writes that before he discovered the doctrine of vocation he tried to be Mr. Fix-It around the house, trying to achieve a feeling of self-sufficiency. But inevitably he would botch the job. "That," he says, "was before I discovered the doctrine of vocation. I have no calling that would authorize or equip me to deal with electrical wiring."[22] It is not that we should never try new things, but we should live within and according to our callings and vocations and aptitudes. And of course our vocation can shift over time. A person can begin life as a teacher and finish as a writer. Or he can begin life as a pastor and finish as a plumber. It is necessary to keep listening to what God is saying about our call and vocation because it can change over time.

The Vocation of Every Christian

This is the way I would put the matter. In terms of vocation, *every* Christian has a primary obligation to fulfill the Great Commandment and the Great Commission. This is "job one." There are secondary callings we may be called to in addition to this — being doctors, lawyers, businesspeople, ministers, parents, etc. But they are indeed secondary callings. Our primary task as persons re-created in the image of Christ is to do the very thing Christ came to earth to do — share the Good News of salvation, healing, the coming Kingdom. There are a variety of ways, venues, and avenues for accomplishing the primary task, and it can be accomplished in tandem with and even by means of the secondary callings or tasks.

Unlike some of the secondary vocations, the primary one lasts throughout a Christian's life. There never comes a time when she is not commanded to love God and neighbor with her whole heart, and to do her best to fulfill the Great Commission. The latter is not just the task of ministers, but rather of all believers. Some subsidiary or secondary vocations can be temporary — raising children, playing professional football, etc. These professions come with built-in "expiration dates." Christians, however, should not be at a loss to answer the question, "What should I do with the rest of my life?" when the period of time for a particular

22. Veith, *God at Work*, p. 139.

secondary vocation is done. They know they are always called to fulfill the Great Commandment and the Great Commission, whatever else they may be doing as well, in terms of their secondary calling in their "second career." Christians should never feel they have no purpose or meaning, even if their original secondary calling or vocation has been completed.

Ars Longa, Vita Brevis: Work as Art, Art as Work

I would like to conclude this discussion about what God calls, gifts, and inspires us to do by talking briefly about a particular profession that Christians need to think better of — the vocation of artist or artisan. I am not going to present a theology of art and its value and place in the Christian tradition, but I do want to present a brief case for being an artist as a proper way to glorify God and edify others.

But perhaps a word is in order first about God as an artist. We can see this just by looking at the stunning beauty of creation, but God is not just a visual artist; God is also an inspirer and creator of music, as Robert Banks points out.[23] For instance, God tells the Israelite leaders in Deuteronomy 31:19, "Now therefore write this song, and teach it to the Israelites." In fact, a direct connection is made between God giving verbal wisdom to someone and God inspiring song in 1 Kings 4:32: "God gave Solomon wisdom . . . he spoke three thousand proverbs and his songs numbered one thousand and five." The precise number of the latter suggests someone took a specific count of the number of times King Solomon was inspired and given lyrics this way.

God, however, is not just a heavenly source of inspiration. God is a blues singer. Thus in Jeremiah 48:31-36 we hear, "Therefore I wail over Moab . . . my heart mourns for Moab like a flute." He also sings joyful anthems and ballads: "The LORD, your God, is

---

23. *God the Worker* (Eugene: Wipf and Stock, 1992), p. 31.

in your midst . . . he will rejoice over you with gladness, he will re-new you in his love; he will exult over you with loud singing as on a day of festival" (Zeph. 3:17). God sings morning music as well as night music: "By the day the LORD commands his steadfast love, and at night his song is with me" (Ps. 42:8). No wonder the natural response to God is music of all sorts, for God embodies and shares all sorts of music.

Robert Banks puts it this way:

> Just as love is not only directed to or expressed by God, since God, as the apostle John says, is love, so is God not only the one who inspires and enjoys music, but also *is* music and song. This makes God the supreme exemplar, as well as the supreme au-thor and audience, of music. This makes God music's chief pa-tron, which is why making music "to the glory of God" is so fit-ting. It is only giving back to what God has given in the first place. It is only recognizing that the musical dimension of life, like the orderly character of the universe, ultimately stems from the musical character of God. In the end we make music not simply because God gives us the capacity to do so or appreci-ates our making it, but because God is inherently musical.[24]

The problem is that we live in a very pragmatic culture. Many people in the contemporary West believe that if something doesn't serve some obvious utilitarian purpose, then it should be seen as superfluous at a minimum, and certainly optional. That sort of practical bent can be seen in some of our famous American quota-tions. Yet I would suggest that some of the most important work anyone could do is work that moves one to be a better person, in-spires one to think about the relationship of truth and beauty and goodness, motivates one to do a better job of glorifying God. And art fits the bill in all these categories.

24. Banks, *God the Worker,* pp. 42-43.

It is an old Latin aphorism — *ars longa, vita brevis:* "art is long, life short." Rembrandt may be gathering dust in his grave, but his enormous painting of the Prodigal Son is alive and well, hanging on a gigantic wall in the Hermitage in St. Petersburg, where it continues to speak to us today. I have spent some hours sitting in front of this gigantic painting, contemplating its meaning, point of view, and nuances. Rembrandt's art lives on and continues to speak for him and to us. Great art continues to inspire and motivate us to be creative, which, after all, was part of the mandate God gave Adam in the first place.

Unfortunately, in a workaholic culture that places an inordinate stress on math and the sciences to the considerable neglect of the arts, art is seen as an extra, not as an essential. Painting, for example, is not seen as a real profession, unless one is painting the walls of one's house to increase its value! Yet Proverbs reminds us that without vision the people perish; their souls shrivel up. Human beings created in the image of God are called to be creators, makers, artisans, not merely doers of any task that someone is prepared to remunerate.

It was not always the case in America that arts and languages (the vehicles to other cultures) were treated as nonessential. I began playing in an orchestra in the third grade, took Spanish in elementary school and Latin in junior high, and we all learned the arts along the way. Not so anymore. We now have institutions called math and science high schools, as if other subjects were so clearly of less importance! And indeed, the whole attitude of the culture has been changed from our being truth seekers to being job seekers. In interview after interview, college freshmen explain that they are taking this or that course, this or that major, so that "I can get a good paying job when I get out." The cost of such pragmatism is that one is in danger of gaining the whole world and losing one's soul.

I love to travel to the lands of the Bible and look at some of the magnificent creations wrought in earlier ages. The immaculately wrought sculptures of Praxiteles, for example, always move me. I ask myself — how have we lost so many of these incredible skills in the arts over the ages? Who could produce Michelangelo's *Pietà* today? Sometimes when I worry about the loss of artisan skills and artistic contributions to our world, I take comfort when I read the story of Bezalel and Oholiab. If you've never heard these names before it is perhaps because no one has pointed out to you that being an artist or artisan is a biblical calling or vocation. Here they are in Exodus 31:1-11:

> Then the LORD said to Moses, "See, I have chosen Bezalel son of Uri, the son of Hur, of the tribe of Judah, and I have filled him with the Spirit of God, with skill, ability, and knowledge in all kinds of crafts — to make artistic designs for work in gold, silver and bronze, to cut and set stones, to work in wood, and to engage in all kinds of craftsmanship. Moreover, I have appointed Oholiab son of Ahisamach, of the tribe of Dan, to help him. Also I have given skill to all the craftsmen to make everything I have commanded you: the Tent of Meeting, the ark of the Testimony with the atonement cover on it, and all the other furnishings of the tent — the table and its articles, the pure gold lampstand and all its accessories, the altar of incense, the altar of burnt offering and all its utensils, the basin with its stand — and also the woven garments, both the sacred garments for Aaron the priest and the garments for his sons when they serve as priests, and the anointing oil and fragrant incense for the Holy Place. They are to make them just as I commanded you."

Bezalel was called to the vocation of being an artist and an artisan, and notice how God equipped him. He filled him with his Spirit, which gave him not just ability but intelligence, and not just intelligence but the knowledge he needed, and not just knowledge but "all craftsmanship." His vocation is described as follows: "to devise artistic designs, working in gold, silver, and bronze as well as in precious stones, and in carving wood," and if that were not enough, "to work in every craft." This is one multitalented artist and artisan, a Michelangelo of his day! But Bezalel was not called to use his craft and knowledge for just any task; he was assigned to make the Tent of Meeting, the ark of the Testimony, including the mercy seat or atonement cover, and all other furnishings of the Tent of Meeting — the gold lampstand, the incense altar, the basin, all the utensils, not to mention the woven garments to be worn by the priests, including Aaron and his sons. Oh, and he was also to produce the anointing oil and fragrant incense for the tent as well. After this last work order I am imagining Bezalel saying, "Holy smokes!" His was the honor of constructing and furnishing the dwelling place of God, and notice that he was not encouraged to use cheap materials, or to go out and buy a trailer made out of pressboard and use it as a tabernacle. No, he was called to use the most precious metals and materials, in order to honor God.

As Gene Veith points out, Bezalel is the very first person in the Bible to be said to be filled with God's Spirit. We are being told that he is inspired, enlightened, enabled to be an artist! This brings up an important point. Sometimes Christians, especially frugal ones, think that the creating of elaborate, beautiful works of art, worth lots of money, is itself either a waste of money or at least not good stewardship, if it is not simply sinful altogether. What this story suggests is just the opposite. The believer should give her very best to God, and indeed it is not a sin to construct beautiful art objects or a beautiful building to the glory of God, which is precisely what is going on in this story. The story of work begins with a gardener named Adam, but the first "inspired" worker in the Bible is an artist and artisan, and we would do well to ponder the implications of that fact. Perhaps creativity, including the arts, is the quintessential way the image of God can mirror the Creator God himself?

Friedrich Schiller, the great German poet, once said that the path to freedom lies through beauty. It must be said that there is some connection between beauty and freedom. I was in the Norman Rockwell museum recently in Rutland, Vermont, looking at one of his most famous paintings. It is a painting of the entryway of a large Gothic cathedral in a major American city, perhaps Rockwell's hometown of New York. One of the workers in the cathedral is standing on a ladder and changing the sign that hovers over the entrance-way doors, announcing this week's sermon. The sermon title is "Lift Up Your Eyes." But on the street below are the commuters, all heads down, scurrying toward their morning jobs.

What a great parable of a workaholic culture, without the time or sense to look up and see the beauty of things that God and his creatures have made! I cannot speak for others, but good art does raise my vision of what the world is and can be. It gives me hope that human beings can live by the better angels of their natures, and not by the demons that drive them, if they will but be transformed by grace. Perhaps if we catch a glimpse in art of something better, something bigger than we have yet contemplated, aesthetics can have an ethical effect on us. And in at least one sense Schiller was right — by being transfixed by the beauty of Christ, we are transfigured and set free. Paul puts it this way: "And we all, who with unveiled face contemplate the Lord's glory, are being transformed into his image with every increasing glory" (2 Cor. 3:18). When we lift up our eyes, and behold true beauty, then in some sense we become what we admire; we become works of the great artisan, the great sculptor of human personality — Christ. And if the Son has set you free to be a work of art, to be your best self, you are free indeed.

CHAPTER THREE

Slackers and Sloths of the World, Unite!

Personally, I have nothing against work, particularly when per-formed, quietly and unobtrusively, by someone else. I just don't happen to think it's an appropriate subject for an "ethic."

Barbara Ehrenreich

The heights by great men reached and kept
Were not attained by sudden flight,
But they, while their companions slept,
Were toiling upward in the night.

Henry Wadsworth Longfellow

Maybe you remember *The Big Lebowski*, the 1998 movie by the Coen Brothers. Its main character, "the Dude," played by Jeff Bridges, is a middle-aged stoner who lives in Los Angeles and does all in his power to avoid any and all work. The Dude is the quint-essential slacker. The film bombed at the box office, but in the years since has become so popular that *Rolling Stone* recently named it the most revered comedy of the 1990s, with fans being known to claim that it "changed [their] lives."[1] How can this be? Andy Greene, who wrote an article about *The Big Lebowski* for a recent issue of *Rolling Stone,* has a theory:

> Early in *Lebowski,* the narrator (a cowboy named the Stranger, played by Sam Elliott) intones, "Sometimes there's a man, who, well, he's the man for his time 'n place." The odd truth is this man — the Dude — may have been a decade ahead of his time. Today, as technology increasingly handcuffs us to schedules and appointments — in the time it takes you to read this, you've missed three e-mails — there's something comforting about a forty-something character who will blow an evening lying in the bathtub, getting high and listening to an audiotape of whale songs. He's not a 21st-century man. Nor is he Iron Man — and he's certainly not Batman. The Dude doesn't care about a job, a salary, a 401(k), and definitely not an iPhone. The Dude just *is,* and he's happy.
>
> "There's a freedom to *The Big Lebowski,*" theorizes Philip Seymour Hoffman, who played Brandt, the wealthy Lebowski's obsequious personal assistant. "The Dude abides, and I think that's something people really yearn for, to be able to live their life like that. You can see why young people would enjoy that."[2]

Many Americans, it would appear, found something enviable in the way the Dude seemingly managed to give up work without giving up happiness. The message of *The Big Lebowski* is tune out, turn on, and be happy. You don't need to be a contributing member of society, or be involved in the work force in any meaningful way. You can be happy by being infinitely self-indulgent and narcissistic and blocking the world out altogether.

Yet as much as the Dude may have become a kind of pop-

1. A. Greene, "Decade of the Dude," *Rolling Stone* (September 2008).
2. Greene, "Decade of the Dude."

culture hero, it is my unscientific guess that the slacker is not nearly so prevalent a character in our society as the sloth. I am thinking here of the person who simply tries to get by, on the job and elsewhere in life, the kind of individual who goes to work every day but would rather win the lottery in order to have the rewards without the effort. How far we have come from the biblical ethic of work, that we admire the person who obtains the ends but sidesteps the means, or who blows off the ends altogether and finds contentment in pleasing himself. How different this vision of life is from that of someone like St. Benedict!

Benedict, the medieval monk, had little time for the lazy or indolent. He believed that good, honest, hard work served as a good prophylactic against evil. He believed strongly in the old saying that idle hands are the Devil's playground. Here is how he put it: "Idleness is an enemy to the soul. Therefore the brothers should be occupied according to the schedule in either manual labor or holy reading."[3] This rhythm of work (or study) and prayer led to the motto of the Benedictines, *ora et labora* (prayer and work). The idea behind this system is that hard work wears the lust of the heart out, or at least keeps the heart and body so occupied that it is too tired for diversions. The concern is that, left alone and idle, even the Christian can fall prey to the lusts of the heart. "Faced with too little to do or too little to read, our soul becomes imperiled."[4] Benedict was not much of a contemplative monk; in fact, he was wary of too much contemplation.

There is something to this theory. There is no doubt that too much leisure time leads to boredom, which leads to wandering thoughts, which can lead to trouble and sin. John Wesley was so convinced of this truth that one of his Forty-four Standard Sermons was titled, "On Wandering Thoughts," and the advice he

3. *The Rule of St. Benedict,* trans. A. C. Meisel and M. L. del Mastro (Garden City: Image, 1975), p. 86.

4. D. H. Jensen, *Responsive Labor: A Theology of Work* (Louisville: Westminster John Knox, 2006), p. 31.

gives in it sounds much like St. Benedict's. It is not an accident that Wesley himself, in his later years, when he found himself lonely and most of those whom he had loved had died, frequently prayed, "Lord don't let me live to be useless." Laziness is not the same thing as rest. Rest is commended in the Bible. Laziness is not. Laziness is an attitude about work, followed by a pattern of behavior, that leads one to try to avoid work — sometimes at all costs. So let us consider the wisdom of Proverbs about "the idler," the lazy person.

Of Sluggards and Sloths (Not the Three-Toed Variety)

Perhaps you remember this guy. The one on your high school relay team who would never run hard, even though he could. Or the girl on your Math All Stars team who was great in practice, but refused to deliver the goods when the heat was on in competition, even though she clearly knew the answers. I think of the guy on my summer work crew with the City of Charlotte Landscaping Division. He came to work drunk and expected the other members of the crew to pick up the slack, mowing parks, graveyards, traffic islands, and the like. He'd sit in the shade while we sweltered in 95-degree heat, and then mow for the last thirty minutes of the day because he knew the big boss would be coming to pick us all up at quitting time. We've all run into this person; indeed, most of us have worked with him or her in one form or another.

Perhaps you've also run into the famous list of the seven deadly sins — that is, those sins considered since the early days of the Church to be particularly serious: lust (in Latin, *luxuria*), gluttony (*gula*), greed (*avaritia*), sloth (*acedia*), wrath (*ira*), envy (*invidia*), and pride (*superbia*). This list has been circulating at least since the time of Gregory the Great (circa A.D. 590), and smack dab in the middle of it is indeed sloth. Who knew that laziness was a serious sin? Well, the author of Proverbs certainly thought so, and in fact this list is in part modeled on biblical texts like Proverbs 6:16-19. It is interesting, however, that the Latin term *acedia* referred originally to unnecessary melancholy or sadness. It was around the time of the Reformation that it began to be seen more as laziness, the opposite of zeal or diligence or willingness to engage in hard work. We can see this in John Bunyan's 1678 classic *Pilgrim's Progress.* His protagonist, Christian, is on a journey to the Celestial City, and along the way he has the following encounter:

> I saw then in my dream, that [Christian] went on thus, even until he came at a bottom, where he saw, a little out of the way, three men fast asleep, with fetters upon their heels. The name of the one was Simple, another Sloth, and the third Presumption.
>
> Christian then seeing them lie in this case went to them, if peradventure he might awake them, and cried, you are like them that sleep on the top of a mast, for the Dead Sea is under you — a gulf that hath no bottom. Prov. 23:34. Awake, therefore, and come away; be willing also, and I will help you off with your irons. He also told them, If he that goeth about like a roaring lion, 1 Pet. 5:8, comes by, you will certainly become a prey to his teeth. With that they looked upon him, and began to reply in this sort: Simple said, I see no danger; Sloth said, Yet a little more sleep; and Presumption said, Every tub must stand upon its own bottom; what is the answer else that I should give thee? And so they lay down to sleep again, and Christian went on his way.

The so-called Puritan work ethic was crystallized in works like *Pilgrim's Progress,* which had an enormous impact on Protestant Christianity in both the Old and New Worlds. Not coincidentally, Bunyan's allegory became a classic with the rise of the Industrial Revolution in the eighteenth and nineteenth centuries, and of course various economic theories have arisen linking Protestantism to the rise of capitalism. Yet only a distorted understanding of the Puritan work ethic could have led to industrial capitalism, for that ethic emphasizes, among other things, that all things belong to God, and that the believer's job is to engage in good, honest labor and to be a steward of God's resources, an approach meant to lead to sacrificial giving, not to making money hand over fist. But I digress. We must reflect on the issue of sloth.

Ancient wisdom literature often featured stock characters — the fool as opposed to the wise person, the sluggard as opposed to the diligent worker. The portrait of the sluggard in Proverbs is at times comical. Consider, for example, in Proverbs 26:13-15: "The sluggard says, 'There's a lion in the road, a fierce lion roaming the streets!' As a door turns on its hinges, so a sluggard turns on his bed. Sluggards bury their hands in the dish and are too lazy to bring them back to their mouths. Sluggards are wiser in their own eyes than seven people who answer discreetly."

This portrayal is quite humorous: the sluggard is someone who makes up excuses in order not to go to work, who sees himself as wiser than others but only fools himself.

But in fact, as Proverbs 6:6-11 makes evident, here is a person who is heading for poverty as he fails to plan ahead. Indeed, he, like the Dude in *The Big Lebowski,* so lives for the moment that the sage in Proverbs says that he needs to go take lessons from ants, who at least have enough sense to store things up for the coming winter. Alas, "the sluggard does not plow after autumn, and so he begs during the harvest and has nothing" (20:4). He is not merely a procrastinator; he is one who avoids hard work at all cost, which is why in Proverbs 12:27 he is contrasted with the man who operates with due diligence and foresight.

Not surprisingly, the sluggard in Proverbs is characterized by his laziness. Consider the following examples:

Like vinegar to the teeth, and smoke to the eyes,
    so are the lazy to their employers. (10:26)

One who is slack in work
    is close kin to a vandal. (18:9)

Laziness brings on deep sleep;
> an idle person will suffer hunger. (19:15)

Do not love sleep, or else you will come to poverty;
> open your eyes, and you will have plenty of bread. (20:13)

The craving of the lazy person [for ease] is fatal,
> for lazy hands refuse to labor.
All day long the wicked covet,
> but the righteous give and do not hold back. (21:25-26)

It's not just that the sluggard takes the path of least resistance; rather, he takes the path of least exertion. His life is one of avoidance — avoidance of things that require real effort or could prove to be challenging. He seems to respond only to real pressure or pain from a taskmaster or overseer.

Derek Kidner offers an excellent summary, worth quoting at length, of the character and traits of the sluggard:

> The sluggard in Proverbs is a figure of tragi-comedy, with his sheer animal laziness (he is more than anchored to his bed: he is *hinged* to it, 26:14), his preposterous excuses ("there is a lion outside!" 26:13; 22:13) and his final helplessness.
>
> (1) *He will not begin things.* When we ask him (6:9, 10) "How long . . . ?" "When . . . ?," we are being too definite for him. He doesn't know. All he knows is his delicious drowsiness; all he asks is a little respite: "a little . . . a little . . . a little. . . ." He does not commit himself to a refusal, but deceives himself by the smallness of his surrenders. So, by inches and minutes, his opportunity slips away.
>
> (2) *He will not finish things.* The rare effort of beginning has been too much; the impulse dies. So his quarry goes bad on him (12:27) and his meal goes cold on him (19:24; 26:15).
>
> (3) *He will not face things.* He comes to believe his own ex-

cuses (perhaps there is a lion out there, 22:13), and to rationalize his laziness; for he is "wiser in his own conceit than seven men that can render a reason" (26:16). Because he makes a habit of the soft choice (he "will not plow by reason of the cold," 20:4) his character suffers as much as his business, so that he is implied in 15:19 to be fundamentally dishonest. . . .

(4) Consequently he is *restless* (13:4; 21:25, 26) with unsatisfied desire; *helpless* in face of the tangle of his affairs, which are like a "hedge of thorns" (15:19); and *useless* — expensively (18:9) and exasperatingly (10:26) — to any who must employ him. . . .

The wise man will learn while there is time. He knows that the sluggard is no freak, but, as often as not, an ordinary man who has made too many excuses, too many refusals and too many postponements. It has all been as imperceptible, and as pleasant, as falling asleep.[5]

It is important to add to all this that the sluggard is not an incapable person, but rather one who makes excuses. For him the chief good in life is relaxing. In this respect he certainly sounds like the Dude. The sluggard has no plans to achieve anything. Life is just too much effort, too hard, too frightening.[6]

Another book of Old Testament wisdom literature, Ecclesiastes, offers a somewhat but not altogether different picture of work. The author of Ecclesiastes sees no apparent purpose to life, so there is a sense in which there is no reason not to seize the day and enjoy life. He points out that the connection between work and reward, or between righteousness and reward, does not appear to be at all inevitable.

While he has no patience with the lazy person, the author of

5. D. Kidner, *Proverbs* (Downers Grove: InterVarsity, 1964), pp. 42-43.

6. For more on this see my *Jesus the Sage* (Minneapolis: Fortress, 1994), p. 27.

Ecclesiastes also recognizes that there are limits to what work can do for us. "For this is your lot in life and in your toilsome labor under the sun. Whatever your hand finds to do, do it with all your might, for in the realm of the dead, where you are going, there is neither working nor planning nor knowledge nor wisdom" (9:9-10). This is a very fatalistic view, in contrast to the positive one we find in Proverbs. There is no teleological character to work in Ecclesiastes. The book is perhaps all too aware of the fact that hard work does not necessarily lead to prosperity or wealth. For Christians, the New Testament adds an important Kingdom context to the words of Ecclesiastes as well as other Old Testament passages that deal with work and wealth.[7] Nevertheless, there is truth to be found in this book, as Leland Ryken writes: "If life is lived only at ground level ('under the sun'), work is a terrible toil, 'vain' and empty, a mere striving after wind."[8]

What strikes me about the Bible's critique of laziness and slothfulness is that it does not merely assume that hard work is the norm. It assumes hard work is a good thing, a way to provide for one's family and one's future. From this perspective, work is thus inherently forward-looking. The Old Testament sage's vision, of course, does not include the New Testament's eschatological sanction for work, working because the end of all things is drawing nigh and there will be accountability at the last judgment for the deeds done in the body, even the deeds of the Christian (see 2 Cor. 5:10). In the New Testament, we work in the light of Kingdom come and for the values that will be on display in full when the Kingdom does come on earth.

---

7. See my *Jesus and Money: A Guide for Times of Financial Crisis* (Grand Rapids: Brazos, 2010).

8. L. Ryken, "Work, Worker," in *The Dictionary of Biblical Imagery*, ed. L. Ryken, J. Wilhoit, and T. Longman III (Downers Grove: InterVarsity, 1998), p. 966.

Workaholics Anonymous

But what of the sluggard's mirror opposite, a character who doesn't really appear in the Bible? What of the workaholic? Granted that "daily work, so far from being a hindrance to Christian living, is a necessary ingredient of it," what about the person who has no life outside his or her work, and who basically does nothing else?[9] American culture has support groups for people with all kinds of addictions: people who eat too much, drink too much, and, yes, even those who work too much. Workaholics have several reasons for their condition: they may be people who simply love their jobs, people who feel they haven't achieved enough in their jobs, people who are unsatisfied with their lives at home, or people who are paid by the hour and simply want to earn more money.

For the Christian person, though, there can be little excuse for such behavior since the Bible tells us that the cycle of work and rest is something God programmed right into the pattern and fabric of human existence, even in the way the week was organized. Rest times, sabbatical times are good things. (Of course, in my profession sabbaticals hardly follow the biblical mandate, because it is expected that a teacher or scholar will have a *productive* sabbatical, usually finishing one or more writing projects. This is hardly resting, or even recharging of batteries. At most it's being given time just to focus on one sort of task rather than ten.)

Even if we view rest as nothing more than an opportunity to recharge and revitalize ourselves so we can go back to working more efficiently and with more excellence, the fact is we need rest each and every day. Someone consistently working eighteen-hour days is someone who is likely to burn out quickly. Burnout is a topic not much discussed in the Bible, though it is certainly a common topic in the church and the larger culture these days. For

9. Alan Richardson, *The Biblical Doctrine of Work* (London: SCM, 1952), pp. 36-37.

Christians, however (and perhaps especially for members of the clergy), burnout is not just a physical or emotional matter; it is also a spiritual matter.

A person who is created in the image of God and re-created in the image of Christ is a person who needs times for prayer, meditation, and other means of communing with God that are not part of her normal vocation. And of course, rest looks different depending on the type of work we do. For someone like me, it means time away from the teaching, committee meetings, and advising students that my job involves. For the parish minister, it means time away from preparing sermons, doing pastoral counseling, and hospital visitations.

In one of the more amazing paradoxes in the Gospels, when Jesus speaks with the voice of Wisdom (Matt. 11:29-30; cf. Sirach 6:19-31), he talks about light burdens and easy yokes in the same breath as he speaks of giving us rest! The state of being heavy laden and weary, the classic description of the person who has experienced the effects that the Fall has on our work, is contrasted with Jesus' light burden and easy yoke. Yet notice what Jesus does not say. He does not say that when a person becomes his follower she exchanges heavy burdens for no burdens, and harsh yokes for no yokes. Indeed, the demands of discipleship are considerable when it comes to the issue of work. It has been said that to come to Jesus costs nothing (the new birth is a gift), but to follow him costs everything. As aphorisms go, this one has the ring of truth to it.

But why would assuming Jesus' yoke and burden be considered light and easy? Is it because one has the satisfaction of knowing one is working for and with the Lord? This may be some of it. Any burden may be bearable if it is believed to be for an ultimate good cause. But I suspect something else is meant as well. I think Jesus is inviting us to be his true yokefellow. (This passage may well be the source of Paul's idea when he calls a fellow minister his true yokefellow in Philippians 4:3, and when he warns about being unequally yoked with unbelievers in 2 Corinthians 6:14–7:1, a comment that is not particularly about marriage although it is often taken that way, but rather about idolatry, the incongruity of being spiritually yoked with unbelievers.)

What I mean by this is that I think that what Jesus has in mind is that we share his yoke and burden, which of course also means the converse — when we are doing Christ's work he is sharing our yoke, or better said, the yoke we have assumed at his invitation! This is what makes the burdens light and bearable; indeed, in the very midst of carrying them one can experience rest, the rest and peace that only Christ can give, which leads to quiet satisfaction and confidence that one is doing the right and good thing, and to peace of mind, and to a host of other restorative benefits.

The Christian cure for being a workaholic has several elements. First, we must repent and recognize that the whole yoke does not fall on our shoulders. As Christians we are burden sharers, not burden bearers. Second, we must realize the necessity of taking times of rest and sabbatical from our primary vocation precisely in order that we may do it well. One of the very reasons so many ministers experience burnout is that they are not taking time to be led by the still waters where the Lord restores their souls. Third, we have to recognize that our work has a goal and a purpose that is a Kingdom purpose, and therefore it is a purpose we do not undertake alone but rather with the whole body of Christ. We should be taking up our tasks realizing that there is promise from God of its proper fulfillment.

It is after all, in the end, the Lord's work, the Lord's ministry, the Lord's task, and he works all things together for good. We do not need to feel the weight of the world on our own shoulders when Jesus, the ultimate Atlas, has already borne that burden and overcome it on the cross and through the resurrection. There is no greater burden, or indeed enemy of all that is good and true and beautiful and alive, than death itself. And Christ has already overcome death. Work, in the light of Easter, should be life-giving, not death-dealing.

Here, however, it is important to emphasize what we have already said: work is a good thing, and a God thing — if, that is, one is doing good and godly work. It is part of our original, intended purpose according to God's design, and in the case of Christian work it must be done in the light of and with the knowledge of the coming Kingdom, the coming divine saving reign of God on earth, when his will shall transpire fully on earth, as it already does in heaven. Kingdom work is a preview of coming attractions when heaven comes down, when Christ returns, and glory fills our souls. Work involves a shared task with Christ, a shared burden; and while we should not be careless, we can be relatively carefree in the knowledge that nothing done in the service of the Lord is in vain or is for naught.

As Christians we should not model ourselves on the slacker, the sluggard, or the sloth, but at the same time neither is the workaholic our paradigm — Christ is. If even God can be said to "cease" in the Genesis story, and if even Jesus says that the Sabbath is made for humankind, not the other way around, then somewhere between the sluggard and the workaholic is the fruitful and faithful servant, the worker who stands approved by the Lord.

CHAPTER FOUR

Call Forwarding and Vocation's Variation

I long to accomplish great and noble tasks, but it is my chief duty to accomplish humble tasks as though they were great and noble. The world is moved along, not only by the mighty shoves of its heroes, but also by the aggregate of the tiny pushes of each honest worker.

Helen Keller

We make a living by what we get, but we make a life by what we give.

Winston Churchill

Paul Minear once said that the Bible is "an album of casual photographs of laborers. . . . A book by workers, about workers, for workers — that is the Bible."[1] This being the case, it is rather stunning that we are able to leaf through most of the major Bible dictionaries and find absolutely no articles on work at all! It is as if the Bible had nothing to say on this subject. Oh, yes, there is plenty of

---

1. P. Minear, "Work and Vocation in Scripture," in *Work and Vocation*, ed. J. Nelson (New York: Harper, 1954), pp. 32-81, here p. 33.

discussion of works of the Law, usually in a negative vein, and usually in the context of the discussion of Pauline material or in the usual debate about Paul and James and the issues of faith and works. But beyond that there is an almost universal silence on work itself, and in particular on work as calling and vocation. It behooves us, then, to examine some of the biblical evidence that has some bearing on this subject more closely. We have introduced the question already, but it deserves more detailed attention.

The story of Moses at the burning bush in Exodus 3 is rich with implications for our study of work. It is a classic call narrative — but if we examine it closely, we will see that it is also the first known example of call forwarding. That is, Moses says to God, in effect, "Here I am, Lord — take somebody else, please!" Moses makes the usual excuses to try to get out of his calling. He belittles himself ("Who am I that I should go?"). He tells God he failed Public Speaking 101. He reminds God of the possible failure of the mission, even the part about talking to his own people, never mind Pharaoh ("What if they do not believe me or listen to me?"). Finally, when God seems insistent on sending Moses, Moses just flat-out says, "Please send someone else" (4:13), making God flat-out angry. This is hardly an exemplary response to God's call; in fact, Moses sounds a little like the sluggard from Proverbs, whom we looked at in the last chapter. At least he is being honest, but it certainly seems there should be more appropriate ways to respond to God's overtures. Yet the Bible is full of this kind of call narrative.

We should note, too, that most of them are not also conversion narratives, though sometimes the two become one. But what is the relationship of call to vocation, especially since the word "vocation" comes from the Latin *vocare* — to call? The answer is simple. Call is the divine initiative. Vocation is what happens when we respond to the call. Vocation is when we take up our work based on the call. Being called, equipped, even gifted is one thing. Responding is another, and we should take care not to pursue any sort of work before we realize we have been pursued, called, equipped, and gifted for such a vocation. This matter is complex, and the truth is that there are as many different calls as there are persons, and almost as many vocations pleasing to the Lord.

One of the more striking and remarkable call narratives I have ever read is that of Barbara Brown Taylor. Taylor went to seminary. But, she says, "I did not have a single clue what I would do when I graduated. I didn't even belong to a church. So I began asking God to tell me what I was supposed to do. What was my designated purpose on this earth? How could I discover the vocation that had my name on it?"[2] She then relates how she sought the proper place and posture to be alone with God so she could hear the answer, finally climbing up a rickety old fire escape no one was supposed to be on. "Then one night when my whole heart was open to hearing from God what I was supposed to do with my life, God said, 'Anything that pleases you.' 'What?' I said, resorting to words again. 'What kind of answer is that?' 'Do anything that pleases you,' the voice in my head said again, 'and belong to me.'"[3] It's that last bit that's the kicker.

You see, if we belong to the Lord, then we know that what truly will please us is the residue of what God has placed in our hearts, what God has meant for us to be. What will be pleasing to the ever-so-carefully molded person, whose mind has been renewed and whose soul has been saved and whose heart has been fixed on the Lord, is of course what will please God. When we belong to God, we are God's servants, the ones who submit to God's will and good pleasure. But notice how God honors Taylor's earnest search, how he lets her know that she does not need to feel boxed in. In fact, she would go on to do many different forms of God-pleasing work.

2. B. Brown Taylor, *An Altar in the World: A Geography of Faith* (San Francisco: HarperOne, 2009), p. 109.

3. Taylor, *An Altar in the World*, p. 110.

Taylor concludes, "Whatever I decided to do for a living, it was not *what* but *how* I did it that mattered. God had suggested an overall purpose, but was not going to supply the particulars for me. If I wanted a life of meaning, then I would have to apply the purpose for myself."[4] It is interesting that Taylor goes on to say, "In a world where the paid work that people do does not always feed their hearts, it seems important to leave open the possibility that our vocations may turn out to be things we do for free. . . . While it is sometimes possible to turn your love into your work — especially if you can figure out how to live on less — that is not always the best idea."[5]

As I said, each person's call and vocation may well be different. For some people their profession, their daily work, is not their vocation, not the main thing the Lord has called them to do, even though any good profession can and should be done in a Christian manner. What pays the bills may not pay the Piper who calls you. This does not mean, however, that doing Christian work should always be pro bono. No indeed, both Jesus and Paul agree that a worker is worthy of his or her hire, including those we call ministers or missionaries. But I am saying that we need to take God's call as it comes and listen closely to his directions.

A lot of well-meaning Christian people try to assemble a good ministry in rather the same way that too many fathers try to assemble their child's first bicycle, that is, without paying attention to the explicit instructions. However gifted a person may be, that person needs to be called and to listen intently to the contours of the call. So let's take a few moments to look at a classic parable of Jesus, one that certainly has to do with our being good stewards in God's vineyard and with how God responds to the ways we use the talents he has bequeathed to us.

In modern English the word "talent" has many resonances,

---

4. Taylor, *An Altar in the World*, p. 110.
5. Taylor, *An Altar in the World*, p. 116.

normally referring to some native ability a person possesses. But in the famous parable in Matthew 25:14-30, from which the English word comes, the so-called parable of the talents, the word has its original sense of a unit of money. In Jesus' day a talent was a very large sum of money: six thousand denarii, equivalent to six thousand days' wages for a day laborer. That works out to about one million U.S. dollars today! If we know this, we know right off the bat that even the man given only one talent was given an enormous sum by his master. But, as the old preacher George Buttrick put it, talent is a two-sided coin. On one side it says "ability," and on the other "responsibility."

The situation Jesus describes in this parable was common enough in antiquity. A well-to-do estate owner goes on a long trip, leaving his household servants in charge to manage things while he is gone. Of course, everyone knows he will return and demand an accounting for what has happened in the interim. In Israel and elsewhere, domestic slaves were allowed to earn money, and they could actually earn more wages and bonuses by managing the master's estate well. So it would be in their own interest, as well as their master's, for slaves to do good work in their master's absence.

Now, one of the keys to this parable comes to light in verse 15: the master gives the talents to the slaves "each according to his abilities." The talent, then, should not be mistaken for ability. It is rather something given to a person to do with his or her abilities. The real issue here is clearly the one of stewardship while the master is absent. And as we learn from the third slave, protecting the master's assets while doing nothing with them is not in any way considered sufficient unto the day.

There is a clear difference between these servants in character and ability. The ones with five and two talents, respectively, immediately go and invest them, but not so the man given just one talent. He does what we might expect someone to do during a period of economic depression — he does not trust moneylenders, and so he digs a hole in the ground and buries the talent with which he was bestowed. This was in fact a fairly common practice in antiquity: people who lived near a temple were often able to deposit their valuables in the temple treasury, but those who lived where no temple was nearby would bury their treasures for safekeeping. It's not an uncommon practice in modernity, either. During the Great Depression, when banks were failing right, left, and center, my grandmother put her money in the hope chest at the end of the bed. But the point of this parable is that God doesn't want what he has given us to go on deposit! He wants it used for Kingdom purposes. He expects us to be industrious.

The master in this parable expects all these servants to invest the money, to step out in faith and do something with it. Doubling one's return was considered a good but normal return on such an investment, and coming back with nothing but the original talent was considered a complete failure to launch, a complete failure to do what was expected. Such behavior was inexcusable, and the excuse given by the one-talent servant is weak — he knows the master to be a demanding person, and so like the sluggard he is more afraid of what he might lose than excited about what he might gain while being the steward of this talent.

Notice now verses 19-23, and the reward for good stewardship. The reward for doing well with the investment is being put in charge of more work, more investments! When the master learns that the five talents have turned into ten his praise is unstinting: "Well done, good and faithful servant. You have been faithful in a few things; I will put you in charge of many things. Come and share your Master's happiness." The reward for good work is more work, but we must bear in mind that while the subject here could be about any kind of good work, the issue is work done how and for whom — in this case work done well and done for the sake of the master. Notice that the praise for the man who doubled the two talents is exactly the same as for the man who doubled five. The issue here is not who makes the most money, but rather what we do with what we have. Notice as well that the outcome involves the master's happiness, in which the workers are invited to share. God is delighted when we do our work well and to his glory and in his service and for his purposes.

Notice how differently the response of the servant with one talent begins, in verses 24-25. He does not begin by saying what he did with the talent. He simply hands the original talent back and starts describing the master's character flaws! This is not the way to win friends and influence people, much less God. The servant characterizes the master as a person who reaps where he does not sow, and gathers where he has not sown seed. In short, he is depicted as not merely an opportunist, but as something of a robber baron. So the brief soliloquy of the least talented servant ends with, "Behold, here is what belongs to you." Several points immediately stand out. First of all, remember Jesus' parable of the man who found a treasure in a field? It would appear that burying the money was no safer than putting it in a bank in antiquity. Second, when a person gives money to a banker to invest, he is not really doing the heavy lifting; the banker is. Thus, the third servant could hardly complain that the work of investing would be too hard for him. Finally, this last servant takes no responsibility at all for his failure to act, for his lethargy. He certainly sounds like the sluggard of Proverbs.

At this report, the master explodes, describing the third servant as both wicked and useless (the Greek word used here could mean either useless or lazy). A useless servant is no servant at all. Notice that wickedness here has nothing to do with misspending, wasting, or losing the talent. What was squandered was an opportunity. Industriousness is one of the major virtues praised in the wisdom literature, just as it is here. Thus, the response of the master means, "You are a bad steward, and since you are lazy, you are useless." Work, and investing ourselves in it, is seen as a good thing by Jesus. In the end, the one talent is taken from the useless servant and given to others: "For those who have will be given more, and they will have an abundance. Those who do not have, even what little they have will be taken from them." Jesus here seems to be modifying the aphorism found in Proverbs 9:9. The underlying principle seems to be that if you instruct and empower the receptive and wise more, they will make good use of it.

Again we must remind ourselves that the subject here is not money, but the tasks, endowments, and work that Jesus gives his disciples to do. It should be stressed, however, that the end of this parable is not meant to teach us that the rich get richer and the poor get poorer and this is the way God intended it to be. The issue is not a bare economic one, but rather how one responds to the tasks, the work, the Master gives a person. And notice that Jesus nowhere gives any money to any of his disciples!

The fate of the useless servant is described at verse 30 in some graphic detail. He is thrown into utter darkness where there is weeping and gnashing of teeth, a metaphorical way of talking about damnation. While Jesus does not teach that individuals are saved by means of their works, he does teach that a person who is already a servant of the Master will be lost if he or she fails to use the talents, to do the tasks given by the Master. More to the point, Jesus does not think salvation is a finished product, short of entering the Dominion at the eschaton; that entering is most certainly affected by the behavior of the servants in Jesus' teaching.

Jesus believes there are in fact rewards in the Kingdom for work well done; when Peter asks about such rewards, Jesus describes family, friends, banquets, even land. Paul suggests that the works of even ministers will be tested by fire, and though one may escape by the skin of one's teeth, there will be no rewards in the Kingdom for those who have "built poorly" (see 1 Cor. 3:5-15). In other words, there are rewards in the Kingdom, but the Kingdom itself is not a reward for services rendered. What this parable definitely suggests is that the relationship of our work to reward and even to salvation is far more complex than those in some Christian circles would like to admit.

Let us conclude by reflecting a moment about what this parable tells us about calling and vocation for the followers of Jesus. First, it suggests that the Master is in charge, we are not, and he assigns the tasks.

Second, it also suggests that he bestows on us tasks according to his assessment of our abilities or giftedness. This is good news, and it is no doubt why we sometimes hear the Christian cliché that God will not hand down more than he knows we are able to handle. But there is another, related factor as well, too seldom considered, that must be mentioned here. The degree and maturity of our faith has something to do with the tasks God gives us and the way we ought to exercise our God-given gifts.

You can see this very clearly in Romans 12:3-6. These verses are often mistranslated, and our concern is with the first and last of these, which ought to read like this: "For I say this to you according to the grace given me, that you not esteem yourself above what it is necessary for you to think, but to think according to sound judgment, each as God has divided the measure of faith." And then, "each having differing grace gifts according to the grace given us, if it is prophecy, prophesy according to the proportion of faith." Various translators have resisted this more literal rendering of these verses because they did not like the notion of God giving some more faith than others, but that is exactly what Paul is saying. Granted, he is not talking about saving faith, he is talking about the degree of actual trust in God one has after conversion, for all his readers are already Christians. Paul's view, of course, is that gifts come from God, and so does the grace and faith to exercise them. Some of this may be a matter of maturity, some being young and weak in faith, others older and stronger, but all have some measure of faith. Paul's deepest concern is that Christians be real about themselves, evaluating themselves with sound judgment, thinking neither too highly nor too lowly of their gifts and abilities. When it comes to prophecy then, Paul says one must be cautious not to prophesy further than one's faith stretches; otherwise the prophecy may be one part inspiration and a further part perspiration. The point is that Christians should exercise their gifts according to the measure of that greatest of all gifts — faith. This requires discernment. Perhaps an example is in order.

We have all met incredibly talented musicians in church, who are at the same time incredibly immature in the faith. Should they be allowed to simply give free rein to their gifts? I don't think Paul would be happy about this, but notice that he places the burden of deciding this issue on the individual — each person must think wisely about his or her maturity or faith or both, or lack thereof, and participate accordingly. What happens when we do not follow this rule? Well, as Ecclesiastes would say, "Vanity!" The individual becomes puffed up instead of the congregation becoming built up. It becomes a self-serving rather than other-serving exercising of one's gifts. Now of course God can write straight even with a crooked stick; he can work against the grain and trajectory of someone if he has to. But this is not how the body of Christ ought to work. It is a good thing for individuals to assess where they are in their faith walk, think about what they have been gifted to do, and then listen carefully to the still, small voice as tasks are parceled out, to figure out what work they are supposed to be doing.

From the parable we discussed above, we learned that the Master rewards industriousness and condemns laziness and use-lessness. Industry, zeal (as long as it is a zeal exercised according to knowledge and good judgment), and hard work are all commended by Jesus.

Finally, Jesus' disciples are always and everywhere stewards of God's work, God's property. They never become owners, nor do they become those who decide for themselves what work they ought to do. They are always assigned tasks by the Master, and the parable of the talents is particularly pertinent for us here and now because it talks about the state of affairs of the stewards of God's estate while he is away in a far country — or, to put it in Christian terms, while Christ is in heaven and before he returns to earth.

That would be now in church history. Blessed will be those whom the Master finds about *his* business when he returns to earth. All of this discussion leads in important ways to our discussion of work not merely as life vocation but as ministry, the topic to which we now turn.

CHAPTER FIVE

Work as Ministry, Ministry as Work

The society which scorns excellence in plumbing because plumbing is a humble activity, and tolerates shoddiness in philosophy because philosophy is an exalted activity, will have neither good plumbing nor good philosophy. Neither its pipes nor its theories will hold water.

John W. Gardner

The secret of joy in work is contained in one word — excellence. To know how to do something well is to enjoy it.

Pearl S. Buck

Work as an Offering to God, a Response to Grace and Salvation

Several years ago I wrote the following poem about work and ministry:

Opus Magnum

Weary, worn, welts on hand
Work has whittled down the man
To the bare necessities
Of what he is, and what he'll be
Was this then his destiny?

Defined, refined by what we do,
The toilsome tasks are never through
Thorn and thistle, dirt and dust
Sweeping clean, removing rust
All to earn his upper crust?

Sweat of brow, and carried weight
Rose too early, slept too late
Slaving, striving dawn to dusk
'Til the shell is barely husk
Staunch the stench with smell of musk?

But work is not the curse or cure
By which we're healed, or will endure
It will not save us in the end,
It is no foe, but rather friend
But while it molds us will we mend?

Task Master making all things new
Who makes the most of what we do,
Let our work an offering be
A timely gift from those set free
From earning our eternity.

When work is mission on the move
By those whose efforts serve to prove

That nothing's wasted in God's hands
When we respond to his commands
Then we shall hear him say, "Well done"
To those who worked under the Son.

What I wanted to convey in this poem is that work can be a calling, a mission, a ministry, an offering to God, and in any case and
at all costs it should never be seen as merely a way to "make a living," which is an exceedingly odd phrase. We might do well to talk
about making a Christian life before we talk about making a living, if what we mean by the latter phrase is making money so we
can survive. All too often, "making a living" really means "making
a *comfortable* living," or even, "making a killing," if we are honest
with ourselves.

From a Christian perspective, all persons in Christ are called
to both ministry and discipleship of various sorts. Labor is part of
this calling, some of which will be remunerative, some of which
will not be. Paul in 1 Corinthians 9 is insistent that ministers of
various sorts should be offered pay for their labors, since Jesus
says that a worker is worthy of his hire, but of course, ministers
can refuse pay as well. If we see work as part of our life stewardship, just as play and worship and prayer and sleep and so many
other things are part of our stewardship, we will begin to be on
the right track.

Life is a gift from God, and work can be a blessing rather than
a curse if it is done to God's glory and for Christ's Kingdom. Work
is part of what we offer to God on a daily basis as we respond to
God's call to do various things that matter in life, even do things
that change life for the better, or even save lives. There are several
keys to a proper Christian attitude about work.

Work should be done in full remembrance that initial salvation or conversion is in the first place a gift of God's grace. It is not
a debt God owes to us. Therefore we can neither work nor worm
our way into God's graces, and we shouldn't ever see work as a

means of doing so, or as a means of making amends, or as a means of atoning for things we've done wrong. Work has no capacity to convert us, nor can it compensate for our lack of salvation, nor can the doing of it make God an offer he can't refuse. However, work done in service to God, as a grateful response to God's grace, can be a great good. It can help feed, clothe, and even save the world. As we have said previously as well, "working out our salvation" that God has worked into us can be said to be part of our work. The will of God for our lives is sanctification, and what we do affects that sanctification (see 1 Thess. 4). And here is where I add that the ultimate expression of holiness of heart and life, the ultimate expression of sanctification, is doing the will of God, which is to say doing the ministry he has called each of us to do. What is interesting is that if we focus on the doing of the ministry, sanctification happens as a byproduct of that focus, but if we focus on ourselves and our sanctification, ministry may never happen. Ministry, you see, is other-directed.

When we reflect on the ministry God calls each of us to do, we should avoid the mistake of our culture, that is, defining ourselves by what we do. We are all creatures created in God's image (which is not an accomplishment but a gift), and if we are Christians we are creatures renewed in the image of Christ. This is who we are. What we do, whether we are doctors, lawyers, scientists, ministers, or theologians, is important, but it does not define or eclipse who we are. We have all met doctors or other professionals who had excellent skills but who were not very good persons. They were good at their tasks but bad at being real human beings, much less Christian ones. It is no accident that Paul, in the Pastoral Epistles when he is talking about ministers, says precious little about what they ought to be doing, and quite a lot about what kind of persons they should be (see, for instance, 1 Tim. 3; Titus 1).

Furthermore, we should not evaluate our work by how much we are paid to do it, nor by the amount of praise, fame, or kudos we garner for doing it. We should evaluate our work by whether we have done it well, done it to the best of our ability, done it honestly and in good time, done it to the glory of God, whatever the human response to the work may be. Unfortunately, we live in a world where many people, even Christians, do not merely define themselves by what they do, but define their true worth by their financial or net worth. This is not only tragic; it gets in the way of finding out who and whose we really are.

Lastly, it is right to take satisfaction from a job done well. This is in itself a reward, but since in the end we are playing to an audience of One, the evaluative voice that really matters when it comes to assessing our work is the one we will one day hear say, "Well done, good and faithful servant." It is no accident that there is a dialectic established in Genesis between work and rest, between work and play, between work and worship. Work should never be a be-all and end-all experience, or else it will indeed be the end of us all, prematurely, as we work ourselves to death.

Not long ago I was visiting the Billy Graham Library in Charlotte. I had finished the tour and was going to leave, but there was one more outside spot to see, the memorial garden for Ruth Graham, Billy's wife. There was a very large tombstone carved with her name and dates, as well as the following words: "Construction Completed. Thanks for Your Patience." When I saw that inscription it dawned on me that there is a whole different way of evaluating work, ministry, and time. What if you evaluate life's work as something God has been doing in and to you? What if you conceive of it as a timed process that takes time? What if "work out your salvation with fear and trembling, for it is God who works in you to will and to do" is viewed as the most important work of all, a work dependent on God's doings in us that we cannot even work out unless God has first worked it in? What if this sort of working is the one that really matters and affects our eternal destiny?

Work as Ministry

With these sorts of general considerations in mind, we can then begin to look more closely at ministry as work, and work as ministry. It will be well, too, if we remind ourselves of a few key points before we turn to some key scriptural texts. First, it was the concept of the priesthood of all believers that motivated Reformers such as Martin Luther to talk about all good work done by Christians as ministry, thus breaking down the distinction between work in general and ministerial work in particular, or between sacred and secular work. I quite agree with Luther on this point. This in turn leads to an understanding that any sort of good life work is a calling that God gives a person, leading to certain tasks assigned according to ability and gifting. The parable of the talents is as applicable to those we call ministers as to those we call laypersons, as applicable to women as to men. Put succinctly, the parable of the talents is for all believers who have the ability to work! This, of course, also means that the Christian is always responsible to God in Christ for what she does with what tasks she has been assigned, and there will be an accounting by Christ when he returns.

What that parable tells us is that Christ is looking for industry, integrity, honesty, loyalty, a striving after excellence, a doing of our tasks to the best of our ability, a taking responsibility for our own actions . . . and we could say more. Regardless of the work a Christian does, it should be seen as a calling, not merely a job, and it should be seen as a ministry done in service of the King and his Kingdom, not merely a task.

The eschatological situation changes the way we view work in this way: now that salvation has been loosed in the world, above all we have the task to do our work in a way that bears witness to that truth and to the one who said he was the Way, the Truth, and the Life. Whether we are talking about lifestyle evangelism or bearing witness by the integrity of our work and work ethic, Christians all know there is a world to be saved, and participating in that is indeed "job one" for all of us. The Lord gave the Great Commission to all the post-Easter disciples, not merely the Eleven. We are to make disciples of all nations and lead them to the point of the ultimate task of all creatures great and small — worshiping the one true God.

Work, then, from a Christian perspective, is not just viewed in light of the original creation order, much less in light of the Fall. It is primarily viewed in the light of the Christ event, and it looks forward to the completion of that event when Christ returns. Christ is returning like a thief in the night (and we have no idea whether that will transpire sooner or later). What this eschatological fact does when it comes to work is that it gives a certain urgency to the basic task of making disciples, either directly or indirectly through our work. But there is more.

What the eschatological horizon also does is make the ordinary or mundane things and tasks of this world be seen for just how contingent and temporary they are. When Paul in 1 Corinthians 7:17-20 and 29-31 reflects on how the Christ event has changed "business as usual" for the Christian, he says this:

> Let each of you lead the life that the Lord has assigned to you, to which God called you. This is my rule in all the churches. Was anyone at the time of his call already circumcised? Let him not seek to remove the marks of circumcision. Was anyone at the time of his call uncircumcised? Let him not seek circumcision. Circumcision is nothing, and uncircumcision is nothing; but obeying the commandments of God is everything. . . . I mean, brothers and sisters, the appointed time has grown short; from now on, let even those who have wives be as if they had none, and those who mourn as though they were not mourning, and those who rejoice as though they were not rejoicing, and those who buy as though they had no possessions, and those who deal with the world as though they had no dealings with it. For the present form of this world is passing away.

Paul is saying, as plainly as he can, that since Christ and the eschatological situation have come, it will no longer be adequate to live on the basis of the old wisdom, the old verities about life and death, love and marriage, possessions and property, work and rest. The things of this world and the people of this world have been put on notice that they have an expiration date. Things will not continue forever the way they have always been. This in turn means that one must recognize the contingency of all of earthly life and its institutions and activities, not because, as the book of Ecclesiastes suggests, all is vanity or meaningless, but because all now must be viewed in light of the really important things in life, namely, salvation in Christ and his coming Kingdom. Even marriage or death pales in significance when compared to these eschatological realities now in play, and they must now change how we view work and rest, marriage or singleness, life or death.

The ultimate upshot of this for the Christian is that the old basic priorities of making a living and providing for one's family and getting ahead in the world have all been relativized, or placed further down the list of priorities, below the more basic and essential task of leading people to Christ and into the Kingdom. As we see from reading 1 Corinthians straight through, Paul does not think those kinds of tasks are just for the paid ministers, either. He is telling the whole audience to think in a new way about their lives, relationships, and work in the light of the divine saving activity of God in Christ that keeps happening in their midst.

He is saying that even things like marriage and children are not and should not be the be-all and end-all of our existence. Marriage is a temporal institution for our earthly good, as Paul makes clear in Romans 7:1-4. When one of its members dies, the marriage is over. Paul simply wants believers to understand the difference between temporal and eternal things, and to make the main thing the main thing. In fact, Paul suggests that with the coming of the Kingdom a calling and a gifting are required to get married, or to be single for the sake of the Lord. He calls it a "charism," a grace gift, to live in either condition in this life (see 1 Cor. 7:1-10). In other words, Christians no longer take the creation order mandate to be fruitful and multiply as their marching orders if they are to fulfill God's purpose for them in life. In fact, Paul suggests that we no longer live on the basis of what comes naturally or seems natural, or even on the basis of the old creation order. Instead, we look at life from a Kingdom perspective, which means that we can see either marriage in the Lord or singleness for the Lord as blessed options, not necessities. Among other things, this view of life allows women to assume all sorts of roles, including those we would call ministerial, which they had no time for before since they were committed full-time to producing offspring and raising them.

The Work of the Ministry of the Word

But what about those who have been especially called and equipped for teaching and preaching, for evangelizing and proselytizing? Paul has some specific things to say about such persons, and clearly he would agree with James's sober assessment that not many should desire to be such educators, as with that task comes more responsibility for the outcome. Let us read 1 Corinthians 3:5-23:

> What then is Apollos? What is Paul? Servants through whom you came to believe, as the Lord assigned to each. I planted, Apollos watered, but God gave the growth. So neither the one who plants nor the one who waters is anything, but only God who gives the growth. The one who plants and the one who waters have a common purpose, and each will receive wages according to the labor of each. For we are God's servants, working together; you are God's field, God's building.
>
> According to the grace of God given to me, like a skilled master builder I laid a foundation, and someone else is building on it. Each builder must choose with care how to build on

it. For no one can lay any foundation other than the one that has been laid; that foundation is Jesus Christ. Now if anyone builds on the foundation with gold, silver, precious stones, wood, hay, straw — the work of each builder will become visible, for the Day will disclose it, because it will be revealed with fire, and the fire will test what sort of work each has done. If what has been built on the foundation survives, the builder will receive a reward. If the work is burned, the builder will suffer loss; the builder will be saved, but only as through fire.

Do you not know that you are God's temple and that God's Spirit dwells in you? If anyone destroys God's temple, God will destroy that person. For God's temple is holy, and you are that temple.

Do not deceive yourselves. If you think that you are wise in this age, you should become fools so that you may become wise. For the wisdom of this world is foolishness with God. For it is written,

"He catches the wise in their craftiness,"

and again,

"The Lord knows the thoughts of the wise,
   that they are futile."

So let no one boast about human leaders. For all things are yours, whether Paul or Apollos or Cephas or the world or life or death or the present or the future — all belong to you, and you belong to Christ, and Christ belongs to God.

Much about this passage calls for comment. First of all, these church planters or apostles or leaders are all viewed as servants of God, and indeed servants of God's people. They are also called *God's co-workers,* and Paul expects them to be honored as such. They are first called planters and waterers of God's field, then builders of God's temple, but it is stressed that it is God who gives the growth, and in both cases Paul means a living entity that is being built up — the people of God.

Notice what this text says — both the planters and waterers have one and the same purpose, and God is the one who will reward them for work well done. They are to do their work with care and leave the results and rewards in God's hands. The judgment day will bring to light what sort of work Apollos or Paul or Peter or others have done, and "if what has been built . . . survives [the fiery test of the judgment], the builder will receive a reward." If, however, the work has not been done with care and not with the right materials, the builder will suffer loss, but will be saved, though as one escaping through the fire. Notice that it is God who is ultimately to judge the builders' work, not the congregation. The leaders belong both to God and to the people, but then all of the people of God belong to and are accountable to God for their behavior. Everything is to be done *coram Deo*, before the face of God, not merely bearing in mind that God is watching, but bearing in mind that God is now working, and also will one day do the quality control test on one's work.

The second thing to stress about this passage is that Paul is not merely telling us that God compels and empowers our ministry. He is saying that God is working at it as well. We are co-laborers with the Almighty, and there can be no higher privilege. God has not merely assigned us a job to do, handed us the tools and ability, and told us to get on with it. The Big Boss is always on the job, and we are working alongside him, which ought to be sufficient motivation not to slack off and to always give our best. It ought also to be an enormous comfort.

William C. Placher reminds us that we should resist the tendency to limit vocation or calling to those who, like a Paul or an Apollos, are evangelists or teachers.[1] I agree with him (and with

1. *Callings: Twenty Centuries of Christian Wisdom on Vocation* (Grand Rapids: Eerdmans, 2005).

Barbara Brown Taylor, as we read in the last chapter) that there should be no one definition of what counts as a calling and vocation for a Christian person. At the same time, we cannot ignore that Paul in 1 Corinthians 3 and 7 and 9 is not simply saying that any good task is just as crucial to the Kingdom work as any other, not least because he relativizes the normal or mundane tasks in life in 1 Corinthians 7, saying we should live "as though not" when it comes to those sorts of matters. Clearly there is no higher calling or vocation for anyone than sharing Christ, though, as I have said, this can take many forms, some direct and others indirect.

Three points emerge from these reflections. First, Christians need to have a priority list. They need to know what is more and what is less important for them to do or work at in life, and this partly depends on what they have been called and gifted to do, or not. Let me give a personal example. While I both enjoy and derive exercise benefit from mowing my grass in due season, it would not be the best use of my time, calling, gifting, or vocation, even during the summer, if I performed this task so incessantly that I neglected my higher calling to write and teach and preach. This would not be an example of me using my talents (literal and figurative) most wisely. Second, we need to be wise enough to see the difference between work of temporal and of enduring value. This requires discernment, and it may require outside advice and wisdom. Sometimes we get far too close to what we are doing to step back and evaluate it critically, and we get far too wrapped up in it to continue to be open to new callings, new directions. Third, our work should not be seen as our atonement for sins past, nor as our means of earning our salvation. Just because we need to view our work in a theological light, as calling and vocation, does not provide a warrant for us to view work in either of these ways. Fourth, obviously, whatever we do, we should only do things that we can do to God's glory and for the edification of others. And we should derive our satisfaction from doing the work well, not from whether or how much we get remunerated. But we need to consider this last matter more closely, and in some detail.

Work for Hire, or Money for Nothing?

The issue of getting paid for what one does is a sensitive one in a workaholic culture such as ours, so much so that people, even Christians, sadly tend to evaluate their eternal worth on the basis of their net worth, or the value of their work on the amount they get paid to do it. This is without question a huge mistake. Some people get paid enormous sums to do pedicures, which is not high on the list of necessary and meaningful tasks in life from a Christian point of view. The remuneration is out of all proportion to the merit and value of the work. And if we think that is ridiculous we should bear in mind that at least in the case of the pedicurist there is a correlation between work and pay, or laboring and remuneration. In too many cases in our culture, the ideal is envisioned as living "the good life" without having to work for it — "money for nothing," as an old hit song puts it. At the opposite extreme is the cliché that suggests "you don't get something for nothing," which, oddly, causes some people in our culture to doubt that salvation could possibly be a free gift.

Let us start this part of our discussion with another parable, the parable of the day laborers in Matthew 20 (I'll give my own translation here):

> For the Kingdom of Heaven is like the landowner who went out early one morning to hire workers for his vineyard. He agreed to pay the normal daily wage and sent them out to work.
>
> At nine o'clock in the morning he was passing through the marketplace and saw some people standing around doing nothing. So he hired them, telling them he would pay them whatever was right at the end of the day. So they went to work

in the vineyard. At noon and again at three o'clock he did the same thing.

At five o'clock that afternoon he was in town again and saw some more people standing around. He asked them, "Why haven't you been working today?"

They replied, "Because no one hired us."

The landowner told them, "Then go out and join the others in my vineyard."

That evening he told the foreman to call the workers in and pay them, beginning with the last workers first. When those hired at five o'clock were paid, each received a full day's wage. When those hired first came to get their pay, they assumed they would receive more. But they, too, were paid a day's wage. When they received their pay, they protested to the owner, "Those people worked only one hour, and yet you've paid them just as much as you paid us who worked all day in the scorching heat!"

He answered one of them, "Friend, I haven't been unfair! Didn't you agree to work all day for the usual wage? Take your money and go. I wanted to pay this last worker the same as you. Is it against the law for me to do what I want with my money? Should you be jealous because I am kind to others?"

So those who are last now will be first then, and those who are first will be last.

We should pay attention to several aspects of this parable. First, it is talking about day laborers, that is, those who are hired day to day, and so must sit in the market square hoping to be picked to go into the fields, because otherwise the chances are good that they and their family will not eat tomorrow. And just as they work day to day, so they are paid day to day — "give us this day our daily bread" is the prayer of the day laborer. The normal pay for a day laborer was a denarius or drachma, and that is precisely what the landowner offers the first workers in this parable.

To the second group hired he offers to pay them "what is right," and he says the same to the next two groups hired as well, but not to the last ones hired.

When grapes are ripe, there is an urgent need to get them picked quickly before they begin to spoil in order to get the maximum harvest. Thus, the owner goes to the marketplace at dawn, then at nine o'clock in the morning, then again at noon, three, and five in the afternoon. He is puzzled to find workers still standing around waiting to be hired at such a late hour, and he asks, "Why have you been standing here all day doing nothing?" Their reply is the simple and obvious one, "Because no one hired us." What a heartbreaking remark! This parable is not suggesting these men were lazy. They were simply unemployed, and it was a clear sign that they desperately wanted to work and earn a crust of bread that they were still in the marketplace near sundown. Nothing is promised to this last group, but they are given permission to go into the fields and work. The life of the day laborer was quite literally a matter of living hand to mouth, and so even a little pay was better than none. From the landowner's point of view, it was essential to do whatever it took to get that harvest of grapes in, in a timely fashion. If this story takes place in either June or September, then sundown would have been between six and seven in the evening, leaving just an hour or two of work for these last workers.

Leviticus 19:13 and Deuteronomy 24:14-15 tell us that it was customary to pay day laborers at the end of each day, so we are not surprised when in verse 8 the owner tells his foreman to call the workers from the field. But then, interestingly, he tells the foreman to pay them in reverse order of their hiring. The last shall be first. Then something even stranger happens — the workers hired last are paid a full day's wage. And so it is not surprising that those hired first expect more than a denarius, having worked as many as twelve hours. Yet they, too, receive a denarius — and begin to grumble: "These workers who were hired last worked only one hour, and *you have made them equal to us* who have borne the burden of the work and the heat of the day." Suddenly we are in an honor and shame situation. Those hired first feel shamed by not being paid more than those hired last, in view of the extra work they have put in. Notice they do not say anything about "equal pay for equal work," though they could have done so, but rather, "you have made them equal to us." The issue is one of honor and identity, and perhaps they felt that they must have been the better workers, since they were hired first.

In verse 13, the owner addresses them as "friends" and reminds them that he has been perfectly fair with them, paying them exactly what they agreed to at the beginning of the day. The issue here is not one of violation of contract, and so not of justice or fairness in that sense. The owner then adds that they should take their pay and go, asking, "Don't I have a right to do what I want with [the rest of] my money [once the debt of contract has been met]? Or are you envious because I am generous?" Generosity, of course, frequently goes beyond justice, and the owner chooses to be generous to those last hired, perhaps because he knows they and their families need to eat as badly as anyone else. The grumblers are therefore reacting to generosity, not to injustice. Of course this parable is not primarily about money matters but about Kingdom matters, and it is true that God's graciousness always challenges those who think strictly on the basis of merit or quid pro quo. Real ministry goes beyond fairness to meeting the need, and no one should be envious when God is generous.

Our interest in this parable is that it upholds the general principle that "the workman is worthy of his hire" (Matt. 10:10/Luke 10:7; cf. 1 Tim. 5:18). The aphorism presupposes a normal connection between work and pay, but what it means depends on which form you follow. Matthew's form says in effect that the workman is worthy of his maintenance, as the Greek word it uses, *trophos*, refers not just to food but to room and board as well. That is, Matthew is talking about a living wage, not just something that allows one to buy food. Luke's form, on the other hand, focuses instead on the contractual aspect: a person is worthy to be paid for what he has been hired to do. First Timothy 5:18 applies this principle particularly to church elders ("workers deserve their wages") and relates it to the principle in Deuteronomy 25:4 that suggests that even an ox should get some benefit from its hard work. Paul in 1 Corinthians 9:7-18 makes perfectly clear that ministers have a right to make their living by preaching the gospel, as a particular extension of the teaching of Jesus about the connection between work and fair remuneration. In fact, he is more demonstrative than that, saying, "The Lord has *commanded* that those who preach the Gospel should receive their living from the gospel" (v. 14).

The specific ministry of the gospel, as portrayed by Paul in 1 Corinthians 9 and elsewhere, is hard work, and work that deserves fair remuneration, not least because it is most directly the fulfillment of the Great Commission, the primary task for every Christian. Here, then, we have crossed the line from talking about all work as ministry of a sort, to talking about ministry as a particular kind of work that deserves remuneration, fair remuneration. Of course the world's priorities will never be the same as Kingdom priorities between now and when the Lord returns, but at least in Christian circles Paul is encouraging Christians to think in Christian ways about the employment of those who get their living by the gospel.

It is of course true that sometimes hard work leads to major remuneration, and then the ethical dilemma comes not in defending the issue of equal pay for equal work, or a fair compensation for crucial work, or the like; rather, the moral burden shifts from the employer to the employee, from the compensator to the one compensated. By this I mean that what we do with what we make is an ethical matter, perhaps more so for a minister than for anyone else. It is not necessary for a person to live a life of conspicuous consumption just because he has been well paid for what he has done. The issue of the accumulation of wealth is a serious one for a Christian, and I have dealt with it at length elsewhere.[2] The point to be made here is that the minister of the gospel has a particular opportunity and responsibility to lead by example when it comes to the matter of what we do with what we are paid or what we earn, and, to be sure, the congregation will be watching.

Sometimes, of course, the congregation expects the minister to appear prosperous, thus providing them with an excuse or reason to live an opulent lifestyle as well, on the theory that they have a right to it, since all good gifts come from God! And it is true that Christians who work hard and honestly do often face the dilemma of doing well, a nice dilemma to have. John Wesley had to deal with this problem with his Methodists at the rise of the Industrial Revolution, so much so that his most used sermon in the second half of the eighteenth century was titled "On the Use of Money." He himself said his goal was to make sure that by the time the grave beckoned he had given away all that he had or owned. What a different attitude from those ministers who spend their time justifying a luxurious lifestyle with so-called "prosperity theology"!

Most Christians will agree that there must be some ethical discernment on their part to figure out what is a good and godly job for them to do. They will perhaps agree as well that work can and should be seen as calling, vocation, even ministry, and that a worker is worthy of his or her hire, and that includes those workers whom we tend to call pastors, ministers, priests, reverends. They will understand that the work they do and how they do it provides a witness to the gospel and the coming Kingdom, and so it can be seen as part of a larger evangelistic enterprise fulfilling the Great Commission. Making a living is one thing, making a life another, and making a Christian life yet a third thing.

But all too few Christians come to the point of realizing that they are called in their work to be culture builders, or ethos cre-

2. See my *Jesus and Money: A Guide for Times of Financial Crisis* (Grand Rapids: Brazos, 2010).

ators. All Christians, even including, perhaps especially including, counter-culture Christians, sometimes take such an antagonistic approach to culture that they approach it purely apologetically, as something to be deconstructed. But what if God has gifted Christians to use their abilities in the fine arts, in the domestic arts, in all creative skills, to build a more Christian world? Andy Crouch has some good things to say on this subject, and so in our next chapter we will interact with him in detail on the subject of culture making from a Christian perspective.

CHAPTER SIX

Seeing the World from the Crouch Position: Work as Culture Making

The first duty of a human being is to assume the right functional relationship to society — more briefly, to find your real job, and do it.

Charlotte Perkins Gilman

Christ against Culture?

Over the years, Christians have taken a variety of stances toward the cultures in which they find themselves living. Some, like those from Holiness, Mennonite, and Amish traditions, often seem allergic to their cultures, with reactions that range from mild to severe. Others seem more comfortable with culture, seeing it as created and sustained by God, if sometimes in need of reform. In his classic book *Christ and Culture*, the theologian H. Richard Niebuhr outlines five basic understandings of the relationship between Christ and culture.

In the first, which he calls "Christ against Culture," Christ and

---

This material appears in another form in an essay entitled "Cultural Pearls," in *The Bible and the American Future*, ed. R. Jewett (Eugene, OR: Cascade Books, 2009), pp. 237-66.

an evil world are seen in fundamental opposition, and Christ calls his followers to retreat from culture. In the second, "Christ of Culture," Christ and culture are viewed as being in harmony, with Christ embodying the best of culture and showing us how to reform the worst of culture. In the third, "Christ above Culture," culture is not seen as fundamentally evil, but nothing in it can save us, for we need Christ's supernatural intervention. The fourth, "Christ and Culture in Paradox," sees human culture as deeply fallen, but not abandoned by God, so Christians still have roles to play in it. In the fifth, "Christ transforming Culture," human culture is seen as fallen, but capable of redemption through Christian shaping of it.[1]

Maybe one of these positions resonates more with you than others; Niebuhr himself advocates the last paradigm, that of Christ transforming culture. On this showing, Christians are enabled to go about the task of building the Kingdom of God on earth. The problem is that the Kingdom of God in the Gospels is not an item on a human to-do list in the present; rather, it is the divine saving activity of God in our midst that changes persons. This is perhaps why Niebuhr was wise enough to entitle his book *Christ and Culture,* rather than *Christians and Culture.* In any case, all too many have assumed since Niebuhr that what is descriptive in the Gospels should be prescriptive for us — our marching orders as Christians, so to speak. In this, I am reminded of William Blake's famous poem on Milton, which was turned into an English hymn:

And did those feet in ancient time,
Walk upon England's mountains green:
And was the holy Lamb of God,
On England's pleasant pastures seen!

1. For more on these various stances, see Niebuhr's book, *Christ and Culture* (New York: Harper, 1956).

And did the Countenance Divine,
Shine forth upon our clouded hills?
And was Jerusalem builded here,
Among these dark Satanic Mills?

Bring me my Bow of burning gold;
Bring me my Arrows of desire:
Bring me my Spear: O clouds unfold:
Bring me my Chariot of fire!

I will not cease from Mental Fight,
Nor shall my Sword sleep in my hand:
Till we have built Jerusalem,
In England's green and pleasant Land.[2]

Blake, of course, was talking about the English vision of building the New Jerusalem in Great Britain, and not accidentally these verses are part of the preface to his poem about John Milton, who furthered the Puritan vision of life and society in his epic poems and writings. Alas, the Puritan experiments in both England and New England bear painful witness to the fact that even the most devout Christians cannot build the Kingdom on earth, much less the New Jerusalem, not even with the fires of a hundred revivals burning bright. But while the Kingdom is a matter of an event or a happening that God produces and we can only receive, can we talk about the lesser task of culture making, and what the Christian responsibility is when it comes to our work in this capacity? "Culture making" sounds a little less pretentious than "Kingdom building," and it is worth discussing with someone who has thought long and hard about Christians and culture making — Andy Crouch.

2. Blake's poem is widely anthologized; see, e.g., W. Blake, *Collected Poems* (London: Routledge, 1905), p. 211.

In a comment on the back cover of Crouch's *Culture Making: Recovering Our Creative Calling*,[3] Christian Smith, professor of sociology at the University of Notre Dame, says this: "American evangelicals in the last hundred years have found it easy to condemn culture, critique culture, copy culture and consume culture. It has been much harder for them to actively and imaginatively create culture. Andy Crouch is out to change that." I like this already.

Evangelical Christians have too often been guilty of various forms and degrees of tunnel vision. One such form, which I will call "missional tunnel vision," views the world as something people need to be rescued from. Ministry, then, involves rescuing the perishing from a world going to hell in a hand-basket. The problem with this vision is that it not merely promotes a lifeboat philosophy about church and Christian life ("we must live within the safe haven!"), but it also grossly underestimates the power of God and his role not merely in the church but in the world. It also ignores entirely the creation theology, which says that God made the world good, and that human society and human work are valued as good from the beginning.

Yes, we sing, "This is my Father's world," but we hardly mean it or understand it. Some of this comes from what Niebuhr would have called a "Christ against culture" approach to life. Some of it comes from a belief that Christ transforms culture, and there is some truth in that approach as well. But what if Christ came to make all things new? What if he came to create culture, and calls us not merely to transform the culture that exists, but even to build new culture? What if it is in the DNA of the church and in the original mission statement about our *work* that we are supposed to be banqueting with the bad like Jesus did? What if it is true that "greater is he who is

---

3. A. Crouch, *Culture Making: Recovering Our Creative Calling* (Downers Grove: InterVarsity, 2008). I offer special thanks to Andy Crouch, who gave me his blessing to quote extensively from his fine book on culture making in order to more adequately reflect and interact with its helpful discussion on work.

in us" (1 John 4:4) than anything else in the world? I am convinced Crouch can help us gain a more holistic and wide-angle vision of work, vocation, ministry.

Let's start with Crouch's definition of culture: culture is what we *make* of the world that God has created.[4] It's not just about high art or architecture. It's whatever we make of the stuff God created, ranging from an omelet to a *Mona Lisa*. Culture always bears the stamp of our creativity, even if, as so often is the case, it appears we are pretty derivative or unoriginal in what we make. We have, says Crouch, this innate design and desire to make something more of what we have been given. It is part of being created in the image of a God who is both Creator and Ruler, both Sustainer and Redeemer.

Crouch goes on to stress that culture is also about what we make of what there is, which is to say, what *sense* we make of what exists. The world requires some interpreting, some explanation. It would appear that we are the only creature on the planet that asks *why:*

> Making sense of the world, interpreting its wonder and its terror, is left up to human beings alone. . . . We *make sense* of the world by *making something* of the world. The human quest for meaning is played out in human making: the finger-painting, omelet-stirring, chair-crafting, snow-swishing activities of culture. Meaning and making go together — culture, you could say, is the activity of making meaning. (p. 23)

Thus far, culture sounds like an exercise in hermeneutics, or interpreting things that already exist, like a movie critic, for example. But in fact, Crouch goes on to insist that culture shapes and reshapes the mere material world that exists. Humans do not merely observe or interpret the world. They construct it, they make it, in

---

4. Crouch, *Culture Making*, p. 23. Hereafter, page references to Crouch's book will be given parenthetically in the text.

various senses of that term. "Culture, not just nature, has become the world that we must make something of" (p. 27).

Crouch quite naturally asks us to consider the sort of work that goes into road building and how it changes things, and not merely the landscape. I have been watching this process for some weeks now. As I drive to work in Wilmore, Kentucky, a whole new four-lane highway is being constructed, and in the process various bits of this or that horse farm are being torn up, vivisected, displaced. Pretty soon one of my favorite horse farms will no longer be beside Harrodsburg Road, because that road will now go well behind the farm. This will make travel to Wilmore quicker and easier and less "windy," and so my trip into work will be different, my purview different, my outlook different. The making that we do, whether we call it work or not, is culture making, as it remakes our world — both the world out there, usually called "nature," and the world within my mind. Work changes the world and imposes a new culture on what previously existed. Culture creating is inevitable for human beings; the only question is whether Christians will meaningfully and self-consciously engage in such activities as part of their "work" and realize that in so doing they are creating a new world.

Crouch points out how the car and the highway system made impossible what had previously been taken for granted, namely, traveling considerable distances on horseback. You can't do that now on a normal highway — it's prohibited, and even if it weren't, there aren't enough inns and horse barns along the way to support such a mode of travel over any considerable distance. Furthermore, even if you tried it, it would endanger the horse, and exhaust fumes from the cars passing by would probably overcome man and beast in due course. This is why even the Amish hitch rides in cars and on trains when they want to go any real distance. The world has been changed by culture-making human work. It is thus no surprise that Crouch concludes, "Without culture, literally nothing would be possible for human beings. To say that culture creates the horizons of possibility is to speak literal, not just figurative or metaphorical, truth" (p. 35). Culture, in this sense, is very broadly defined and not to be associated just or even primarily with the high arts. (I have to say, however, that my mother the pianist would entirely resist calling the building of an interstate highway "culture making"!)

What this means, in plain and simple terms, is that work, our work, Christian work, creates a world, and without hard work even the fulfilling of the Great Commission would be just a nice idea. Grace is conveyed to other human beings through work. Grace and works were not meant to be seen as sparring partners in an eternal theological boxing match. They were meant to be seen as partners in a rowboat, both pulling in the same direction. Likewise, Christianity should not be set over against culture; it should ever and always be set in motion to create culture and worlds.

One of the real problems with Christians is that we can be too insular, living in our own little bubble, and this trend has only accelerated with the enormous rise to prominence of home-schooling and Christian schooling in this country. If all you ever do is sing in the choir or preach to the choir, how is that culture making and world changing in anything like a Christian sense when we are called to make disciples of all nations? Consider again what Crouch says:

> Culture requires a public: a group of people who have been sufficiently affected by a cultural good that their horizons of possibility and impossibility have in fact been altered, and their own cultural creativity has been spurred, by that good's existence. This group of people does not necessarily have to be large. But without such a group the artifact remains exclusively personal and private. (p. 38)

In our culture we tend to think that things as deeply personal as religious beliefs ought to be private matters, but this will never do for an evangelistic religion. We have to become both gospel sharers and culture makers, and the latter involves work. Indeed, our work, if we are not preachers, teachers, or priests, may largely consist of culture making in the most basic of all senses, senses that would not be perceived by most as involving sacred tasks. Christianity, in order to be truly Christian, has to go public, has to become a shared public good, not merely a private self-help program for the already convinced.

One of the most convincing points Crouch makes is that family is perhaps the most elemental and crucial culture-making institution in a society. What goes on in a home need not stay in a home, but in the milieu of a home and in the context of a family all sorts of positive cultural constructions happen. Cooking, for example, is a form of work that is not only culture making but Kingdom making, if you invite people over for dinner, or have some of your Christian meetings in homes, or even if you just engage in friendship evangelism in such a context. "Family [including Christian family] is culture at its smallest — and most powerful" (p. 45). If you don't believe this, go rent the movie *My Big Fat Greek Wedding*.

It is of course true that any talk about changing a whole culture or changing a whole world is in most cases overly ambitious. When John Wesley, who had quite the work rate, said, "The world is my parish," some people believed him, and not primarily because he had already been to Georgia and back. But when we talk about making our work something that is culture making in a way that is glorifying to God and edifying to others, we have to talk about economies of scale. Here is how Crouch puts the matter:

> finding our place in the world as culture makers requires us to pay attention to culture's many dimensions. We will make something of the world in a particular ethnic tradition, in particular spheres, at particular scales. There is no such thing as

"the Culture," and any attempt to talk about "the Culture," especially in terms of "transforming the Culture," is misled and misleading. Real culture making, not to mention cultural transformation, begins with a decision about which cultural world — or, better, worlds — we will attempt to make something of. (p. 48)

One of the most important insights to be gained from the study of culture is the dawning recognition that those who chase the will-o'-the-wisp called new/fresh/trendy will be forever changing and not having much enduring impact. Crouch rightly warns, "There is an inverse relationship between a cultural layer's *speed of change* and its *longevity of impact*. The faster a given layer of culture changes, the less long-term effect it has on the horizons of possibility and impossibility" (p. 56). Those who follow the fads will find that growth may happen in a church or in a business with hard work, but whether they are accomplishing something of lasting value is another question — a question we as Christians must always ask about our work: Is my work of some lasting value? Did it make a difference? Was it worth doing in the first place, or was it in vain? Did this work have some meaning, some purpose, and if so what was it? Of course, answering such questions is not always easy, as the impact and quality of some pieces of work may not be visible for years to come.

When a tenement house collapsed in Miami, Florida, without any apparent provocation or cause, the investigation led to the conclusion that, while the building looked fine on the outside, twenty years earlier it had been built poorly and with inferior materials. It could not have passed a stress test, had one been administered. Disposable culture in a disposable society with all too rapid change is rightly criticized for having little long-term value. Crouch is emphatic about this: "Nothing that matters, no matter how sudden, does not have a long history and take part in a long future" (p. 57).

Change and Culture

It is eye-opening and indeed a little depressing to realize that it is possible to change things for the worse quickly, whereas making things of value or changing things for the better almost always takes considerable time. For example, think of the terror attacks of September 11, 2001, and how rapidly the World Trade Towers fell into dust. But how long did it take to construct them in the first place? Or to clean up after the devastation? Or consider a great work of art like Michelangelo's *David*, which took months to carve, but could be destroyed in the blink of an eye if someone took a hammer to it. Buildings, works of art, even human lives are easily destroyed. Take time to read the lament of the vendors, sycophants, and clients of Rome in Revelation 18 with its refrain, "It all happened in a hour."

We need to realize that our American culture is addicted to "the latest" and assumes that the latest is the greatest and the newest is the truest. But alas, the latest is quickly yesterday's story. Crouch reminds us:

> So hope in a future revolution, or revival, to solve the problems of our contemporary culture is usually misplaced. And such a hope makes us especially vulnerable to fashion, mistaking shifts in the wind for changes in the climate. Fads sweep across the cultural landscape and believers invest outsized portions of energy and commitment in furthering the fad, mistaking it for real change. (p. 58)

Perhaps, then, more emphasis should be put on the work of culture making by Christians, and less on the hope that some future revival will change the world. Crouch quite rightly takes on those who think the way to change the world is simply to change the worldview of the world, on the theory perhaps that "as a man thinks, so he is."

The problem with this is that new thinking is not the same as new doing, is not the same as going to work and changing things. Thoughts must be embodied in deeds, and this takes hard work. If you merely change the thoughts going on inside the horse's head, you by no means have changed the direction the horse is heading — you have to turn the head itself! The problem with so much Christian worldview talk is that we suffer the paralysis of analysis — we spend so much time analyzing our thoughts and our behaviors that we never get around to changing either one. Culture is not just about thinking. It's about doing, and so it is about our work. Crouch reminds us,

> Embodiment may not flow as naturally from thinking as many books on worldview imply. The cartoonist Sidney Harris's most famous drawing shows two scientists standing in front of a blackboard covered with a series of equations. In the middle of the equations is written, "Then a miracle occurs." One scientist says to the other, "I think you need to be more explicit here in step two." When we say, "The Christian vision can transform our world," something similar is happening. Is it really true that simply perceiving the radical comprehensiveness of the Christian worldview would "transform the world"? Or is there a middle step that is being skipped over all too lightly? . . . The danger of reducing culture to worldview is that we may miss the most distinctive thing about culture, which is that *cultural goods have a life of their own.* They reshape the world in unpredictable ways. . . . The language of worldview tends to imply, to paraphrase the Catholic writer Richard Rohr, that we can think ourselves into new ways of behaving. But that is not the way culture works. Culture helps us behave ourselves into new ways of thinking. (pp. 62-64)

What Crouch is making us see here is that the only way to change the cultural landscape is to make more of it, of a variety you endorse. It is never enough simply to change people's ideas about the culture (their worldviews), though that's a start.

For example, the Amish are famous for their pacifism, and part of this involves a belief that people should not carry handguns. Many ordinary Americans also dislike handguns, but if you go and visit Amish country in eastern Ohio and western Pennsylvania you will discover that Amish folks don't just sit around and discuss how bad it is to have handguns around where children and others might be accidentally harmed, which discussion would be followed by various nodding heads. No, they've actually banned handguns in their communities, a rule they enforce rigorously.

Go spend time in an Amish community and you will be in a culture, an ethos, an environment that *is* handgun free. Unless an outsider shows up in their community toting a handgun, no one is going to get shot with such a thing, no strawberry stand is going to be robbed with such a thing, no Amish hardware store is going to be terrorized with such a thing. And anyone who made an idle threat about using a gun might well be taken and confined to the interior of a composting toilet for a while until they regained their senses. Ideas and worldviews alone don't change the world; behavior and hard work do. Cultural change happens when a new way of doing things displaces the old way of doing things.

Crouch reminds us that merely condemning or critiquing culture seldom changes things much, unless someone has something better or more compelling to put in its place. Sometimes what Christians do is simply copy culture and think that will change the world. Consider the evolution of the Christian rock music industry.

Christian rock musicians are hardly ever out there leading the cultural trends; in fact, mostly they are following them, only changing the lyrics. I remember the day when you could go into a Christian bookstore where there were Christian albums and cassettes and there would be signs over the bins saying things like "X sounds like Led Zeppelin," or "Y sounds like Crosby, Stills, and Nash." Alas, it was almost always the case that X and Y were not only less filling, but didn't taste as great, either. Imitation may be the most sincere form of flattery, but it's still imitation rather than adequate creation. Christian musicians needed to learn to gain their own voices, make their own music with a high degree of creativity and skill and excellence.

Nowadays Christian indie and hip-hop artists continue to borrow heavily from the musical styles and even fashion senses of the secular mainstream culture. I used to work in the Christian music business, and back then we would always be thrilled when a Christian artist like Amy Grant would "cross over" into the mainstream. We thought maybe finally the mainstream could be transformed by the Christian message this way. Alas, it didn't happen.

One of the tasks Christians must take seriously in the twenty-first century is culture making, dedicating their work and energies to creating culture that will be winsome and habit-forming to those not already a part of it. And as Crouch warns, creativity, not knock-off imitation, is in the long run the only viable way to change a culture. Christians must work hard to produce the best art, the best movies, the best neighborhoods, the best restaurants, the best athletics possible, not merely by copying, but by coming up with something fresh, new, interesting, life-changing.

And lest we despair, we have a track record of having done it before. For example, consider the coffee culture. You may think Starbucks invented the coffee culture, but actually coffee was first brewed in Ethiopian monasteries and then was exported north and west. The very word "cappuccino" refers to the Capuchin monks whose habits are the same color as this brew. Coffee is a Christian beverage in origins, but you'd never know it today.

Creating a Culture

Crouch is not suggesting that we start from scratch. Culture is cumulative; it keeps building on and recycling from the stuff that existed before. "When it comes to cultural creativity, innocence is not a virtue. The more each of us knows about our cultural domain, the more likely we are to create something new and worthwhile" (p. 73). Thus, Crouch says that real culture making begins with the cultivation of the good things a culture already has and does. We don't need to completely reinvent the wheel to create good new culture. Rather, we need to become fluent in the good aspects of the cultural tradition we are already a part of, and nurture those aspects. We also need to sift the wheat from the chaff and affirm the wheat.

Having spent a good deal of my life making music or listening to it, I can tell you that making music well requires an enormous amount of practice and discipline. Creativity that makes a lasting impact, work that makes a difference, is seldom a matter of sheer spontaneity or mere native talent. If Christians truly want to make an appealing and winsome culture that may actually attract people to Christ, it will require hard work, discipline, and practice, practice, practice:

> So underneath almost every act of culture making we find countless small acts of culture keeping. That is why the good screenwriter has first watched a thousand movies; why the surgeon who pioneers a new technique has first performed a thousand routine surgeries; and why the investor who provides funds to the next startup has first studied a thousand balance sheets. Cultural creativity requires cultural maturity. (p. 76)

Are there options for Christians other than cultural capitulation, accommodation, or rejection to whatever degree? Crouch thinks there are, and he reminds us that even Christians who practice homeschooling and generally avoid the more obviously objectionable forms of modern culture are nonetheless cultural beings. Indeed, even the Amish don't entirely avoid mainstream culture. I have a wonderful picture from when I lived in Ashland, Ohio, of an

Amish buggy stopped at the takeout window at McDonald's. Indeed, many Christians with separatist tendencies do still drive cars, watch television, go to movies, attend sporting events, and the like. This is at most selective rejection of a dominant or secular culture.

Nor can the church simply withdraw from the dominant culture, especially if it wants to continue to bear witness to that culture. Crouch reminds us that

> fundamentalist Christians, like modernist ones, indulged in an attractive but specious distinction between the church and the culture. Their unspoken assumption was that "the culture" was something distinguishable from their own daily life and enterprises, something that could be withdrawn from, rejected, and condemned. In this respect they were just as modern as everyone around them, in accepting too uncritically an easy distinction between the "sacred" and the "secular." This distinction, which served liberals by carving out a sphere of public life that did not have to entangle itself with religion and religious controversies, served fundamentalists by assuring them that it was possible to eschew "secular" pursuits altogether. (p. 85)

This may be the only thing fundamentalists and liberals may agree on about culture. There is a place and a time to condemn culture (think Nazi or apartheid culture), to critique culture (think art that promotes anti-Christian values), to copy culture (think of some of the good contemporary Christian music has done, which largely follows and copies the larger musical trends), and to consume culture (participating in the good aspects of our culture). All of these things can be part of our work and works as Christians. What Crouch is calling us to is creating culture, which is not identical to any of these aforementioned activities. In fact, he offers a clarion call for us to be what God called Adam and Eve to be in the first place — creators and cultivators of all that is good, true, and beautiful in the world, wherever one finds it.

Creatio ex Nihilo?

Most of the creativity Crouch is talking about is not creation "out of nothing," the way God created the world, but a making of things out of preexisting materials. No one would mistake a beautiful saltpeter-glazed water pitcher for a mere lump of clay, but that is where it came from. The middle term was the potter who fashioned that wet lump of clay into something it had no capacity to be, left on its own. It takes intelligence, skill, and, yes, imagination to create culture well, though all too often today we just stress the imaginative aspect when we use the word "creativity." I often wonder what would happen if people approached their normal work with intelligence, skill, and creativity. Of course some do, and sometimes remarkable tasks are accomplished and remarkable things are made.

When I was in Singapore I was given a non-battery flashlight. No, it did not have a solar cell. No, it did not have an electrical plug. It was in fact rather like one of those hand flexers you use to strengthen your hands. From time to time you just squeezed it, using mechanical energy to power the light bulb in it. It was a flashlight that did not need a constant infusion of artificially produced or chemical energy. It created no waste.

God in fact expects creativity out of us, not least because we are created in God's image. Crouch points to the example in Genesis 2 of how God brings the animals to Adam and asks Adam to name them. Of course God could have named them and given Adam the zoological dictionary, but he doesn't. He wants his human creatures to participate in the creative act. This is part of Adam's initial work (p. 108).

> In order for humankind to flourish in their role as cultivators and creators, God will have to voluntarily withdraw, in certain ways, from his own creation. He makes space for the man to name the animals; he makes room for the man and the woman

to know one another and explore the garden. He even gives them freedom, tragically but necessarily, to misuse their creative and cultivating capacities. . . . God's first and best gift to humanity is culture, the realm in which human beings themselves will be the cultivators and creators, ultimately contributing to the cosmic purposes of the Cultivator and Creator of the natural world. (p. 109)

I remember the days before air conditioning. I remember sleeping on the wooden floor in front of the open front door on a hot, humid summer night in Wilmington, North Carolina. You hoped for a breath of a breeze in the morning, but this particular morning not only was there none, but you could have cut out a piece of humidity from the air on the front porch and eaten it! When air conditioning came along to beat the heat, all manner of Southerners like me said, "Huzzah!" The world can be a wilderness for humans unless we cultivate it, unless we create things to help us cope with it, unless we turn a tangled mess into a garden. This is what Crouch is calling us to, and he is saying that it is the primeval task God gave to us in the first place. We must make something out of our world, not merely admire it. While Nature may abhor a vacuum, I do not abhor a vacuum cleaner, as ordering, cleaning, beautifying, creating is part of the human task.

In one of his more interesting insights, Crouch points out that while God meant Adam to be a gardener and ruler, the Snake tempted him to be a consumer rather than a creator and cultivator. "We can only sigh with disappointment as Adam and Eve swallow, so to speak, the idea that a fruit could bring 'wisdom,' even as we recognize how adroitly contemporary advertisers persuade us of equally unlikely results if we will just consume their cosmetics, cars, or cigarettes" (p. 113).

As it turns out, what being in the image of God means is not only that we have the capacity for personal relationship with God in a way that other creatures do not, but also that we, like God, have the capacity to be mini-creators, makers of culture, cultivators of gardens, and equally creators of chaos (as in the Tower of Babel story in Genesis 11).

Perhaps the most helpful insight of all offered by Crouch is the following:

> Jesus had a profoundly cultural phrase for his mission: *the Kingdom of God*. It is hard to recapture the concept of *kingdom* in an age where monarchs are often no more than ornamental fixtures in their societies, if they exist at all. But for Jews of that time and place, the idea of a kingdom would have meant much more. In announcing that the Kingdom of God was near, in telling parables of the Kingdom, Jesus was not just delivering "good news," as if his only concern was to impart some new information. His good news foretold a comprehensive restructuring of social life comparable to that experienced by a people when one monarch was succeeded by another. The Kingdom of God would touch every sphere and every scale of culture. It would reshape marriage and mealtimes, resistance to the Roman occupiers and prayer in the temple, the social standing of prostitutes and the piety of Pharisees, the meaning of cleanliness and the interpretation of illness, integrity in business and honesty in prayer. (p. 138)

Kingdom as Creating Culture

As it turns out, if we truly want to understand work from a Kingdom perspective, we must look at it the way Jesus did. If the Kingdom of God is coming to town, this is so much more than saying a new ruler or sheriff is coming to town, the better to reinforce preexisting laws and rules. No, this king is coming to town to clean house, to set up and cultivate a new way of structuring social life, and thus to create a new culture — a culture of conversion, new creation, and all that that implies. The interesting thing about this is that the chief work, at least at the outset, was the re-making of humankind. The cultural artifacts Jesus was most interested in remolding and retooling and reforming were human beings themselves. He did not come chiefly to be a carpenter, or to build a new Temple, or to construct a new political system or party, or to introduce a new line of clothing or art or food. He came to breathe new life into human beings. No wonder Paul was to call him the new Adam. But after one becomes a new creature, what then? What does work, making culture, look like after that transformation?

Consider the Last Supper, the Garden of Gethsemane, the Cross. The work that Christ chiefly came to do was not a doing, but a suffering. Unlike Adam in that first garden, Jesus did not come to consume but to be consumed. He did not come to do his own will but the will of God. He did not come to eat of a tree that would bring knowledge and death but rather came to be nailed to a tree, the fruit of which would be death, but then life (p. 141).

> Of all the creators and cultivators who have ever lived, Jesus was the most capable of shaping culture through his own talents and power — and yet the most culture-shaping event of his life is the result of his choice to abandon his talents and power. The resurrection shows us the pattern for culture making in the image of God. Not power, but trust. Not independence, but dependence. The second Adam's influence on culture comes through his greatest act of dependence; the fulfillment of Israel's calling to demonstrate faith in the face of the great powers that threatened its existence comes in the willing submission of Jesus to a Roman cross, broken by but also breaking forever its power. . . . In the kingdom of God a new kind of life and a new kind of culture becomes possible — not by abandoning the old but by transforming it. Even the cross, the worst that culture can do, is transformed into a sign of the

kingdom of God — the realm of forgiveness, mercy, love, and indestructible life. (pp. 144-45)

One of the things Christians often seem oblivious to is that they are bearing witness, and making culture, whether they realize it or not. Every people group has a presence, an ethos, a way of making something of the world, and Christians are no different. They see themselves as a family of faith, and like any family they have their struggles and differences. Christians will be more often judged by the way they live in the world, and what they make of the world, than by their overt witness. They will be judged by, among other things, their work ethic — do they work hard, do they come to work on time, do they accept hardship without complaining, do they have honesty and integrity?

The world, the fellow workers, and the foreman are watching. And Christ will be honored or not by how we perform and what we do with the world while watching eyes are upon us. If all we ever do is complain about things, including about our culture's problems, people will notice that as well. We might as well wear T-shirts reading "Buzz-kill for Jesus" if that's what we make of and do with the world.

I suspect that one reason Christians don't see themselves as makers of culture, even when they are at work, is that Christianity is supposed to be a universal religion, a one-size-fits-all religion, a body of believers of every tribe and tongue and people and nation, rather than one with specifically cultural practices, like Judaism or Hinduism. Christians seem to think real Christianity is trans-cultural just because it is multi-ethnic. This, however, is not so. The various different forms of Christianity all have their own ethos, their own way of making culture, their own way of making sense of the world, and their own way of creating an environment within their larger culture where things Christian can happen and prevail, including, of course, worship. And worship is supremely an expression of culture making. African

American worship often looks very different from middle class suburban praise worship. What we need to understand is that whether we are at our job or we are at worship in our church, we are at work constructing a culture and helping to advance the cause of the Kingdom — or not.

Indigenization: Can You Dig It?

A key word for a Christian to understand is "indigenization." Christianity has the ability to be indigenized in many different cultural expressions and still be Christian. Crouch puts it this way:

> As the scholar Lamin Sanneh has pointed out, this translatability sharply differentiates Christianity from Islam, which requires the Qurân to be read in its original language. The gospel, even though it is deeply embedded in Jewish cultural history, is available in the "mother tongue" of every human being. There is no culture beyond its reach — because the very specific cultural story of Israel was never anything other than a rescue mission for all the cultures of the world, initiated by the world's Creator. (p. 155)

It is precisely "translatability" and "indigenization" that make it possible for a Christian to assume most any good job worth doing and work most anywhere. There is a freedom in being a Christian that other religious groups do not have, precisely because Christianity "works differently," because it constructs culture differently, and because it is able to adopt and adapt the best of many cultures and still be true to the essence of its character and credo.

Suppose we did Christianity again the early church way, by which I mean, what if we took seriously that we are family, and we took care of one another? What would happen in a culture of rising unemployment if the church took care of, shared the burden with its widows, its orphans, its unemployed? What if a community of Christians not only did this, but were welcoming to strangers and were prepared to go the extra mile to help them as well? Suppose once again church became a sanctuary and a safe haven, not just a place where we as God's sheep meet, greet, bleat, eat, excrete, and retreat?

Before and during the Middle Ages, Christians provided the doctoring and nursing to strangers during epidemics when the pagan priests and medics had fled the major cities. Christians provided the food, clothing, and shelter for the poor. They did not pass these responsibilities off on the government. They were proactive and created their own worlds of work and service. They stuck together, and lived and died together during the plagues, the famines, the natural disasters such as earthquakes. They had no governmental assistance and waited for no insurance companies to bail them out or to rebuild. They simply rolled up their sleeves and did it.

The church had no magic or medicine to cure the plague, but it turns out that survival even of a terrible disease has a lot to do with one's access to the most basic elements of life. Simply by providing food, water and friendship to their neighbors, Christians enabled many to remain strong enough that their own immune systems could mount an effective defense. [Rodney] Stark engages in some rather macabre algebra to calculate the "differential mortality" of Christians and their neighbors compared to pagans who were not fortunate enough to have the same kind of care — and concludes that "conscientious nursing *without any medications* could cut the mortality rate by two-thirds or even more." The result was that after consecutive epidemics had swept through a city, a very disproportionate number of those remaining would either have been Christians or pagans who had been nursed through their sickness by

Christian neighbors. And with their family and friends deci-
mated by the plague, it is no wonder that many of these neighbors, seeking new friends and family, would naturally convert
to Christian faith. The church would grow not just because it
proclaimed hope in the face of horror but because of the cultural effects of a new approach to the sick and dying, a willingness to care for the sick even at risk of death. (p. 156)

In our current economic crisis, the church has once more the
chance to make and change culture, to build a world, and to bear
better witness to the Christ who said, "inasmuch as you have done
it unto the least of these, you have done it unto me" (Matt. 25:40).

The New Jerusalem as Cultural Artifact

What if Revelation 20–22 is telling us that in the Kingdom humans and their culture will be purified and rescued? What if we
are being told that not just nature and human nature get an upgrade, but also human culture? Crouch says that the fact that the
story ends with a city, the ultimate cultural artifact, points in this
direction. And notice it is a city that is built by taking the things of
nature, and transforming them into cultural artifacts — gems become jewels in the Kingdom, and the bounty and best of human
products are brought into the city to celebrate the return of the
King.

I suspect Crouch is right that the world to come will not be as
drastically different from our own world as we might expect —
it's just that there will no longer be the shadow of sin, sickness,
and sorrow, disease, decay, and death. And I would suggest that
there will be plenty to do as well — for instance, picking the fruit
from all those trees along the central river that will require no
more bug spray or artificial anything. We're going all natural in
the Kingdom, all glorious, and all the best of humanity and its

culture. Notice how nature flourishes in the middle of the New Jerusalem, how nature is incorporated into the eternal city. We will not have to choose between urban and rural, here and there, now and then. It will all be present at once and available to all.

In his discussion of Revelation's ending, Crouch finally collects his thoughts on human work and its importance, its potential to last and make a difference. Listen to what he says:

> We should ask the same question about our own cultural creativity and cultivating. Are we creating and cultivating things that have a chance of furnishing the New Jerusalem? Will the cultural goods we devote our lives to — the food we cook and consume, the music we purchase and practice, the movies we watch and make, the enterprises we earn our paychecks from and invest our wealth in — be identified as the glory and honor of our cultural tradition? Or will they be remembered as mediocrities at best, dead ends at worst? This is not the same as asking whether we are making "Christian" culture. "Christian" cultural artifacts will surely go through the same winnowing and judgment as "non-Christian" artifacts. Nor is this entirely a matter of who is responsible for the cultural artifacts and where their faith is placed, especially since every cultural good is a collective effort. Clearly some of the cultural goods found in the New Jerusalem will have been created and cultivated by people who may well not accept the Lamb's invitation to substitute his righteousness for their sin. Yet the best of their work may survive. Can that be said of the goods that we are devoting our lives to?
>
> This is, it seems to me, a standard for cultural responsibility that is both more demanding and more liberating than the ways Christians often gauge our work's significance. We tend to have altogether too short a time frame for the worth of our work. We ask if this book will be noticed, this store will have a profitable quarter, this contract will be accepted. Some of these

are useful intermediate steps for assessing whether our cultural work is of lasting value, but our short-term evaluations can be misleading if our work is not also held up to the long horizon of God's redemptive purpose. On the other hand, knowing that the New Jerusalem will be furnished with the best of every culture frees us from having to give a "religious" or evangelistic explanation for everything we do. We are free to simply make the best we can of the world, in concert with our forebears and our neighbors. If the ships of Tarshish and the camels of Midian can find a place in the New Jerusalem, our work, no matter how "secular," can too. (p. 170)

In the World but Not of the World, or Otherworldly?

The issue of Christians and their work and their culture making can in one sense be boiled down to the issue of how Christians are to live *in* the world, without simply becoming *of* the world. How is this nice little walk along a high wire, without falling off on either side, achieved?

One way Christians have done it in America, surprisingly enough, is to simply baptize American culture and call it good, and embrace it as their own — with liberty and justice and hot apple pie for some. This has led to odd distortions of the gospel, such as the "prosperity gospel" or the "health and wealth gospel," which suggest that God blesses those he loves with material wealth. This situation reminds me of the old *Pogo* cartoon strip in which Pogo returns from a battle to report to his general that things are not going well. He says, "I have seen the enemy, sir. The enemy is us." The church, it seems, has been more changed by culture than culture has been changed by the church, no matter how hard we work at it.

This is one reason I love to take my students on cross-cultural trips to the lands of the Bible and deliberately take them to places where they will contract cultural vertigo — say, for instance, standing in the magnificent temple in Luxor, staring at hiero-glyphics while overhearing the Muslim call to prayer from the nearby mosque, and watching with one eye a group of Japanese tourists clicking photos on the right and a group of Germans lis-tening intently on the left. When cultural vertigo is suddenly con-tracted, most Americans look for comfort food. I remember one trip when our guide pointed my students to the other side of the road and said, "And there is the American Cultural Embassy." We all turned our heads, and there was a McDonald's — and some of my students were beginning to drool. No wonder we Christians haven't much changed our culture — we love it too much just like it is, warts, wrinkles, and all. But what a sad commentary on America that one of the few universal cultural objects we have managed to export to the world is the Big Mac!

In order to upgrade things in a Christian way and become culture makers in a positive sense, we need to ask the right ques-tions. Crouch suggests we start with these:

> *What is God doing in culture?*
>
> *What is his vision for the horizons of the possible and the im-possible? Who are the poor who are having good news preached to them? Who are the powerful who are called to spend their power alongside the relatively powerless? Where is the impossible be-coming possible?* (p. 214)

The 3 . . . the 12 . . . the 120: On Changing Culture

It is an old cliché that all politics is local, and like most clichés there is both some truth and some inaccuracy to it. But I do think it is true to say that all work is local, and most work actually ac-complishes something when it is done in tandem with other peo-ple, sometimes with only a few other people, sometimes with many. Crouch reminds us that most anything worth doing starts small, including if the work we are engaging in is culture making. Talking about the influence a circle of 3, then 12, then 120 can have, he puts it this way:

> The essential insight of 3:12:120 is that every cultural innovation, no matter how far-reaching its consequences, is based on personal relationships and personal commitment. Culture making is hard. It simply doesn't happen without the deep investment of absolutely and relatively small groups of people. In culture making, size matters — in reverse. Only a small group can sustain the attention, energy and perseverance to create something that genuinely moves the horizons of possibility — because to create that good requires an ability to suspend, at least for a time, the very horizons within which everyone else is operating. Such "suspension of impossibility" is tiring and taxing. The only thing strong enough to sustain it is a community of people. To create a new cultural good, a small group is essential. (p. 242)

What is most striking about this point is that it describes the way Jesus set about to change the world — with an inner circle of three disciples (Peter, James, and John), and a slightly larger circle of 12, and then after Easter a group of 120 (Acts 1:15) when the church was about to be birthed. Now, Crouch does not arrive at these three numbers on the basis of analysis of the Bible, but rather on the basis of a sociological analysis of how cultural change and culture making actually transpire in the vast majority of cases. It starts small and branches out, like the ripples in a pond from a small stone thrown into it. The good news about this is that all work that really matters and makes a difference starts small and locally. Consider the example of Mother Teresa of Calcutta. She did not advertise. Even so, eventually the world beat a path to her door.

Perhaps you remember the movie *Six Degrees of Separation,* whose premise is based on the theory that we are only six persons away from being in touch with all six billion people on the planet. There is considerable truth to this, and what it proves is that networking and work on the internet can have influence right across the globe in ever-widening circles. This is one of the reasons I keep a blog, which involves no advertising dollars at all, but is freely available to anyone in the world with an internet connection. The internet is the greatest culture changer and re-arranger in my lifetime. It has had both positive and negative consequences. For instance, it has been the ruination of my much beloved music shops, and in fact may be the ruination of major record labels and the production of the CD format eventually, since increasingly people just download particular songs that they like.

Christian work, calling, vocation, or ministry that is oblivious to cultural change and is clueless about being a culture maker may not be labor done in vain, but it is certainly labor that is not maximizing what can be accomplished for the Lord. This is one of the things that make Crouch's eye-opening book so crucial. He provides us with a window on how the world works, and doesn't work, when it comes to culture making and cultural change. Crouch is right to stress, however, lest we miss the point, that it is not just all about networking. It is ultimately about creating community, the body of Christ. The goal of all ministry and mission is to increase the size of the body of Christ, so more people will be in right relationship with God and fulfilling their destiny to love God and neighbor wholeheartedly.

I completely agree with Crouch when he says that the sacred-versus-secular dichotomy doesn't work when it comes to defining Christian work. Any work that is good and godly, any work worth doing, can be done to the glory of God and for the help of human-kind. And while we are at it, any such work is full-time ministry.

The religious or secular nature of our cultural creativity is simply the wrong question. The right question is whether, when we undertake the work we believe to be our vocation, we experience the joy and humility that come only when God multiplies our work so that it bears thirty, sixty, and a hundredfold beyond what we could expect from our feeble inputs. *Vocation* — calling — becomes another word for a continual process of discernment, examining the fruits of our work to see whether they are producing that kind of fruit, and doing all we can to scatter the next round of seed in the most fruitful places. (p. 256)

This whole discussion brings to mind a quote from my friend Tom Wright, who says,

If we are to be Kingdom-announcers, modeling the new way of being human, we are also to be cross bearers. This is a strange and dark theme that is also our birthright as followers of Jesus. Shaping our world is never for a Christian a matter of going out arrogantly thinking we can just get on with the job, reorganizing the world according to some model we have in mind. It is a matter of sharing and bearing the pain and puzzlement of the world so that the crucified love of God in Christ may be brought to bear healingly upon the world at exactly that point. . . . Because, as he himself said, following him involves taking up the cross, we should expect, as the New Testament tells us repeatedly, that to build on his foundation will be to find the cross etched into the pattern of our life and work over and over again.[5]

The psalmist has some good and sobering words to offer as we end this chapter on work and culture making. He tells us that un-

5. N. T. Wright, *The Challenge of Jesus* (Downers Grove: InterVarsity, 1999), pp. 188-89.

less the Lord builds our house, our labor is in vain (Ps. 127:1), or, in the words of Psalm 90:17, that we ought to pray that the Lord will establish the works of our hands, make them of lasting value. The true test of the value of something is not merely whether it stands the test of time, but rather if it stands the testing of the Lord, a test that all of our works will one day undergo (see 1 Cor. 3). Work worth doing in the world must be work about which the Lord says, "Well done, good and faithful servant, inherit the Kingdom."

CHAPTER SEVEN

New Balance: The Relationship of Work to Faith, Rest, and Play

> *The trouble with gardening is that it does not remain an avocation. It becomes an obsession.*
>
> Phyllis McKinley

> *A man is not idle because he is absorbed in thought. There is a visible labor and there is an invisible labor.*
>
> Victor Hugo

Faith versus Work?

Separating the sacred from the secular is a recipe for disaster when it comes to thinking about the relationship between faith and work. This is because work is typically assumed to be in the secular category, and the question of the relationship of one's work to one's faith is left hanging, or worse, we assume there is no connection. This becomes especially problematic for people who take a "once saved, always saved" position, assuming that once a person is saved, her behavior and work really don't affect her salvation one way or another. And theologians are guilty of aiding and abetting this problem. David Jensen puts it this way: "If Christian theology avoids the topic of work, then it suggests that the bulk of the Christian life — time spent working — is peripheral to the heart of the faith."[1]

But Jensen unwittingly contributes to the problem when he adds, "Human work can never detract from or add to the work God has already accomplished,"[2] essentially arguing that our work is merely a response to God's (hence his title *Responsive Labor*). The problem with this is that it undervalues our work. We are in fact the body of Christ on earth, and when we do our work aright, it is the work of God, the work of Christ we are doing, empowered by the Spirit, inspired by the example of Christ, guided by the Word of God. Paul is even prepared to go so far as to suggest that his own work, which has led to his suffering, is "filling up the sufferings of Christ" (Phil. 1:29), so closely does he associate our work with even the work of Christ on the cross.

Doubtless God could have chosen to redeem the world and bring in his Kingdom without us, but he has not chosen to do that. He has chosen to use us as his instruments to do his work. Our work, then, if it is good and godly, can never be seen as merely a response to the work of God, though it is often that as well. The work of God can be hindered or helped, added to or destroyed by what we do. Paul is perfectly clear about this when he exhorts the mostly Roman Christians in Romans 14:20, "Do not, for the sake of food, destroy the work of God." Nowhere is the point made more clearly than in 1 Corinthians 3:9: "for we are God's co-workers." Or listen to Ephesians 2:10: "For we are what he has made us, created in Christ Jesus for good works." Yes, indeed, there is a connection between God's work and our work, and it is not merely that we respond to God's work, nor even that God's work in us enables us to do good works, though both of those things are true. While it is go-

1. D. Jensen, *Responsive Labor: A Theology of Work* (Louisville: Westminster John Knox, 2006), p. 2.
2. Jensen, *Responsive Labor,* p. 2.

ing too far to say "God has no other hands than ours" (Dorothee Sölle), it is true that God has chosen to use the hands, arms, feet, wills, and compassion of his people to work out his will on earth.

Jensen is right, however, that to define work as "anything we get paid to do" is too small and narrow a definition of work:

> This reduction of labor to pay, however, excludes the vast array of work that is chronically overlooked or deemed secondary by those who write the paychecks: caring for children, cleaning house, tending a garden, all the domestic activities that occupy our lives without monetary compensation. . . . Defining work as paid labor ignores much of the world's work and marginalizes millions of workers.[3]

One of the worst byproducts of capitalism (which, of course, has some good byproducts as well) is that we are taught to evaluate work not on the basis of its goodness or its usefulness but on whether it is well remunerated. Work's "worth" in our culture is based on its exchange value, not on the basis of its actual usefulness in the eyes of God. This becomes especially obvious when we consider the ridiculous amount of money professional athletes are paid, simply for entertaining us by playing a game. Even brain surgeons and the President of the United States are paid less than many, many sports stars. It's absurd, but this is what happens when the worth of something is judged on the basis of what someone is willing to pay for it and how high the demand for it is. But fallen human beings desire and long for all sorts of worthless and even immoral things. The high demand for sugary soft drinks that have no nutritional value tells us nothing about whether such things should be made or whether they should be consumed. Our economy is based on demand, on desire, on lusts and longings, and on needs, not all of which are either good or good for us.

3. Jensen, *Responsive Labor*, p. 2.

Work as Problem and Pathology

One of the problems we have in coming to grips with our attitudes about work is that work in the computer era has changed for many people, and not necessarily for the better. Many people's experience of work today is much like the comic strip *Dilbert*, where in cartoon after cartoon we meet people working in little cubicles, far removed from their employers, perhaps even alienated from them, chained to endless mind-numbing computer tasks, many of which are purely bureaucratic. There is a reason both my children find this strip so humorous — it rings true to their experience, for both of them work in such cubicles on such tasks every day.

It is interesting that what creates job satisfaction in such an environment is not primarily better pay or regular raises, though that helps, but rather (1) repeated infusions of appreciation for what one does by one's superiors; (2) the possibility of and encouragement to consider mobility and retraining — one is not stuck in one's current task for the foreseeable future; (3) recognition of one's gifts and graces, and the providing of educational opportunities to become a better, more skilled, or more diversified worker.

What these three factors have in common is that in each one, the worker is treated in a personal way, as a person who has potential and abilities. If work is connecting rather than isolating, if work leads to good, positive relationships rather than to alienation, it can be fulfilling and lead to job satisfaction. Many people stay in jobs that they could have left behind simply because they enjoy what they are doing and enjoy the people with whom they get to work. Work, when it creates a team or even a community that believes it is doing something important for the world's good, is not mind-numbing or soul-stealing. It reminds me of a recent commercial for ESPN in which "Billy Moore" shows how individuals can watch sports at work on their computers, and the responses of the two employees are all too revealing: "Sports at work is way better than work at work!" says a man, and a young woman says,

"Now my job is way less soul-crushing." Needless to say, these are very negative stereotypes of work and what gets done at "work."

At the other extreme from life-giving and stimulating work is work that not merely wears people out but stresses them out and leads to serious health problems, and sometimes even death. Yes, there are people who work themselves to death, not least because they have not learned the principles of the cycles of work and rest, work and play, that are needed to be a good and fruitful worker. Work without faith and trust in our fellow workers, our employers, and our work itself can lead to various pathologies and diseases of mind and body.

One of the points that Jensen rightly stresses that helps us to have a Christian orientation toward work is that, as Christians,

> We can never be reduced to our individual labors. The true source of our identity is not our job, but the God who adopts us as children in Christ's name. We do not create ourselves in work. God has already created us in love; our work is — in part — a response to God's creative love. We are not who we are because of what we do, but because of whose we are.[4]

There is great truth in this, but it is not the whole truth, because God did indeed create us to work and for good works, and our re-creation in Christ is also in part in order that we might do good works. Then, too, the hammer shapes the hand. It is true that what we do shapes our identity, not merely our sense of identity.

Cultural Myths about Work: Consumed by Consumption

One of the myths that Jensen is concerned to disprove is the notion that work makes us free, or at least free enough to consume

4. Jensen, *Responsive Labor*, p. 11.

and find an identity. Though in a loose sense "we are what we eat," this really doesn't tell us a lot about our identity. There is a big problem when at the core of our identity is shopping or consuming. When we are consumed with consuming, our identity is not enhanced but rather diminished. If we define ourselves by our appetites and needs, we will have an impoverished view of ourselves.

Another myth is that in the technological age we are likely to have more free time. On the contrary, the "oddity of technological advances in each generation (internal combustion engine, electrical appliances, computer, and email) has been that the very devices designed, at least in part, to reduce human labor have actually created more work!"[5] Americans have responded to "labor-saving" technologies with more work, and thus it is small wonder that two-thirds of us feel overworked (and underpaid). Take the phenomenon of email, and it is a phenomenon. In the 1990s I began to have a trickle of email. Today, on a normal day, and not counting junk mail, I probably have fifty emails to deal with. Imagine if your physical mailbox at your house or apartment regularly presented you with fifty letters a day, ranging from the trivial to the crucial! However we cut it, I spend far more time on the computer these days than I did twenty years ago, and yet I am still expected to do the same amount of lecturing and other professional activities as I did before. The good news about labor-saving devices is that they take some of the Fall, some of the toilsomeness out of our labor. The bad news is that by making labor easier they make labor more apt to be undertaken. "Progress" — another slippery word — has not insured less work; it has insured more.

One of the more interesting factors Jensen comments on is the disappearance of holy days and the reduction of holidays in our calendars. One estimate indicates that in the high Middle Ages, even the hardworking peasant worked only 180 or so days in

5. Jensen, *Responsive Labor,* p. 12.

the year, whereas with the coming of the Industrial Revolution we work much more, well over 300 days of the year! We seem to assume, as Jensen puts it, that "I am busy, therefore I am."[6] But the secularization of work, the workplace, and the week has taken its toll on all of us, and the first casualty was rest and restoration, celebration and community-building time. The United States, as it turns out, is the only developed nation that does not have a law mandating vacation days for workers. Even workaholic Japan requires employers to give their employees 25 days off per year.

One study showed that in 2001 the average American worker worked at least 1,978 hours in a year, or about 325 minutes every single day of the year. There are 1,440 minutes in a day and 525,600 minutes in a normal year, or 8,760 hours. If we subtract from this 2,555 hours of sleep (averaging seven hours a night), that leaves 6,205 hours. This means that in 2001 we were spending at least a third of our time working, and this does not account for time spent on meals, on commuting, and the like.

As Jensen shows in some detail, the reason we have upped our work rate and productivity is because since 1950 we have wanted to consume more. And needless to say advertisements stimulate more and more consumption. Long ago Dorothy Sayers hit the nail on the head when she said, "A society in which consumption has to be artificially stimulated in order to keep production going is a society founded on trash and waste, and such a society is a house built on sand."[7]

One of the reasons why we have some of these profound theological and ethical problems with work is because we are not properly valuing the worker who does the work. As Jensen rightly points out, all workers are created in the image of God and as such must be treated as persons, not merely as means to an end:

6. Jensen, *Responsive Labor,* p. 14.

7. Dorothy Sayers, *Creed or Chaos?* (New York: Harcourt, Brace, 1949), p. 46.

A Christian understanding of work emphasizes the intrinsic value of the worker first and foremost. Valuing the worker — above profit and above efficiency — is essential not merely because each worker is uniquely and irreplaceably created in God's image. The value of the workers reflects not merely the work they do, but is grounded in the persons they are, and whose they are, God's.[8]

Several points emerge from this insistence on valuing the worker. Christian employers must treat their employees as persons created in the image of God. This includes paying them a decent, living wage and treating them with understanding and compassion. The Christian employer knows that we are all God's creatures, and God is watching.

Consider, for example, what Paul says to masters about their relationship with their slaves in Ephesians 6:7-9: "Render service with enthusiasm, as to the Lord and not to men and women, knowing that whatever good we do, we will receive the same again from the Lord, whether we are slaves or free. And, masters, do the same to them. Stop threatening them, for you know that both of you have the same Master in heaven, and with him there is no partiality." I would suggest this provides a very high ethical standard for Christian employers, who are called upon to value their employees and treat them well.

Or consider Leonard Abess Jr., a CEO of a bank in Miami. The *Miami Herald* of February 14, 2009, told a revealing and surprising story about him:

> After selling a majority stake in Miami-based City National Bancshares last November, all he did was take $60 million of the proceeds — $60 million out of his own pocket — and hand it to his tellers, bookkeepers, clerks, everyone on the payroll. All

8. Jensen, *Responsive Labor*, p. 101.

399 workers on the staff received bonuses, and he even tracked down 72 former employees so they could share in the windfall. For longtime employees, the bonus — based on years of service — amounted to tens of thousands of dollars, and in some cases, more than $100,000. At a time when financial titans are being paraded before Congress to explain how they blew billions on executives' bonuses even as they received a taxpayer bailout, the big-hearted banker's selfless deed stands out.

"I retired seven years ago, and all of a sudden I get this wonderful letter and phone call," said Evelyn J. Budde, who spent 43 years at City National Bank of Florida, rising to vice president. "I was shocked," said William Perry. In 43+ years at City National, he climbed from janitor to vice president. Like many longtime City National employees, he forged an unbreakable bond with the bank that continued into retirement. Perry returns regularly for the annual employees' dinner.

Abess didn't publicize what he had done. He didn't even show up at the bank to bask in his employees' gratitude on the day the bonus envelopes were distributed. He was inundated with letters soon afterward. Asked later what motivated him, Abess said he had long dreamed of a way to reward employees. He had been thinking of creating an employee stock option plan before he decided to sell the bank. "Those people who joined me and stayed with me at the bank with no promise of equity — I always thought someday I'm going to surprise them," he said. "I sure as heck don't need [the money]."

This sort of behavior, as opposed to that of those CEOs who take million dollar bonuses when their companies are tanking and employees are being laid off right, left, and center, is what should define Christian employers. Of course it is true that the bank in question had to first be successful and make money for this to even be possible. But the standard to which a Christian employer should be held is that "to whom more is given, more is required or expected." As Christians we have to take the position that we have been blessed in order to be a blessing to others, including in the workplace. And it should be clear that one way to have good, motivated employees is to give them a stake in the company and its success. Putting the success or failure of a company not just in the hands of the owners but also in the hands of the employees is a proven strategy for motivating employees to work hard and to care about the quality of their work. Quality should be "job one," but quality normally only happens when workers are treated with respect, when their work is valued, and when they have a stake in what happens to the products being produced and to the company. An employee stake in a company means that the worker has more than just a paycheck to think about, and it also means that the relationship between employer and employee becomes more of a partnership rather than just one person working for another. When employee satisfaction grows, productivity tends to increase, and workers tend to stay with a company longer, avoiding the expense of having to constantly train new workers.[9]

The Matrix of Work

We should say something here about the interconnectedness of work. Take, for example, the bagel I ate for breakfast this morning. How did I come by it? Of course, in the ultimate sense all good gifts come from God, even our daily bread, as the Lord's Prayer tells us. But the more proximate causes of my having this particular bagel for breakfast involve a staggering amount of people and work. In the first place, there was the farmer who planted and harvested the wheat that went into the bagel. Then there was the miller who turned the wheat into flour. Then there was the baker who turned the flour into a bagel. Then there was the packager

---

9. Rightly, Jensen, *Responsive Labor,* pp. 101-2.

who bagged up the bagels. Then there was the marketer who sold the bagels to the grocery store. Then there were the employees of the grocery store where I bought the bagel, including the cashier and bagger who checked me out.

But that is hardly all. Like most people, I like my bagels toasted, but where did the toaster come from, since I didn't make it? Well, I bought it at a store, where it was delivered after being manufactured in a factory, out of metal and plastic parts made somewhere else. But that is still not all. In order to toast the bagel I had to have electricity to power my toaster. And that's another whole world of workers! I think you catch my drift. God could provide us with manna from heaven directly in response to the prayer for daily bread, but instead most of the time he chooses to use his human servants.[10]

The interconnectedness of work and its products can be demonstrated with virtually any item, and it is a salutary reminder to all of us who tend to think of ourselves as individual consumers, or as people who "support ourselves" and are self-sufficient — all these ideas being modern American myths founded on the even bigger myth of radical individualism. It is good to remember the interconnectedness of all work and all workers in various ways — we need and depend upon each other.

Work and Rest: A Theology of Enough

One of the most pervasive pathologies in our culture today is the tendency to work to excess, without proper rest. Indeed, many workers in America are paid bonuses for doing this — it's called overtime. If this were a rare exception to the normal cycle of work and rest, that would be one thing. The parable of the day laborers suggests that there is a time and a place to put in extra work on a

---

10. See G. E. Veith, *God at Work* (Wheaton: Crossway, 2002), pp. 13-14.

given day. But a good and efficient worker is an alert and rested worker, and this is all the more true in crucial service industries like police, fire, and hospital work. Of course many of us have learned this pattern of overwork not merely on the job but in school, especially all sorts of graduate and professional schools where the mantra is "sleep is optional."

While I disagree with much of Jensen's theological analysis, I quite agree with him that work and rest need to be balanced.[11] Even from a purely utilitarian point of view, you want workers who are rested and well enough to do the job well. Rest is not optional; it is mandatory, and indeed mandatory each and every day of our lives. There is a good reason why we spend about a third of our lives resting or sleeping — as mortal persons we need to do so. This is why I support the idea that any full-time employee should have paid vacation time. All other civilized, developed nations have laws guaranteeing such time, and so should the United States.

But another key to having sufficient rest is, of course, to downsize and downscale our material expectations in life. One of the major motivations in America for doing more work is to up our style of living, to super-size our car, our house, our possessions. While it may be popular, this is not a good motive for doing more work if we already have enough when it comes to all the basic necessities of life.

Paul has some very direct and helpful things to say about a theology of sufficiency or "enough." When he was under house arrest in Rome, he received aid from his friends in Philippi, and he was grateful for it. But then he adds, "I have learned to be content with whatever I have. I know what it is to have little, and I know what it is to have plenty. In any and all circumstances I have learned the secret of being well-fed and of going hungry, of having plenty and of being in need. I can do all things through him

11. Jensen, *Responsive Labor*, p. 108.

who strengthens me" (Phil. 4:11-13). Christians need to cultivate this whole attitude, especially when it comes to material things.

One of the things that characterizes advertising in this country is that it seeks to create "wants" and "needs" where they did not exist before. Most of us need to simply stop listening to all the siren songs that play on our televisions, especially if we already have what we need to live a normal human life. We need to cultivate not craving but contentment. What is the secret of being content in any and all situations? It is knowing that endurance is possible through the strength the Lord gives us. And not merely endurance but contentment is possible, because we have the Lord and the resources he brings when he comes into our lives. You will not hear the prosperity preachers preaching, "Godliness with contentment is great gain." They are interested in other sorts of "gains" too often.

When Bishop Francis Asbury met with his Methodist preachers at their annual conference meeting in Baltimore, it was his regular task to appoint these preachers to their various itinerant circuits all up and down the East Coast of the United States. One minister, who was being sent to northern New England in the middle of December, asked the bishop during the meeting, "What bounty do you give me for going there?" His response was not, "Salary now and pension and retirement later." Instead, he said, "Grace here, and glory hereafter." While all of us need food, clothing, and shelter, if we are primarily working for things that are luxuries and far from necessities in life, we are working for the wrong reasons, and in the wrong ways to the wrong ends. If we have a theology of "enough" and believe that God's grace is sufficient, and we believe God will indeed take care of our needs as we put ourselves in God's hands and do his work, then we should and can come to have a very different outlook on work.

One of the things I have learned of late is that the phrase "brain drain" needs to be taken more literally. I have discovered that those whose work is highly cerebral, while they may be sitting in a chair all day, can end up being consistently exhausted at the end of the day. This is because the more active thinking a person does, the more calories he burns up; indeed, a thinker can burn up more calories than some manual laborers in a day. Here is a basic breakdown of things in a sample case:

If you weigh 180 pounds, your results might look like this:

Totals: 3,130 calories in 24 hr

Sleeping	588 calories in 8 hr
Office Work — general	980 calories in 8 hr
Driving — light vehicle	
(e.g., car, pick-up)	163 calories in 1 hr
Food — preparing, at home	204 calories in 1 hr
Eating — sitting	122 calories in 1 hr
Taking a Shower	82 calories in 30 min
Cleaning — house or cabin, general	122 calories in 30 min
Shopping — groceries, with cart	94 calories in 30 min
Walking — with dog	122 calories in 30 min
Running — 6 mph	408 calories in 30 min
Dressing and undressing	82 calories in 30 min
Watching — TV or movie	163 calories in 2 hr

Notice that the largest single category is "work" calories burned, and we can definitely up the percentages of "work" calories burned if a person is doing an intellectually stimulating job. While most people would see burning more calories as a good thing, if a person is constantly burning the calories at both ends at work, doing too much work, too much overtime, then that person's health is bound to suffer.

Two of my friends who teach New Testament have suffered from chronic fatigue syndrome, one of them having to be medicated for months. What happened? Too much researching, reading, writing, grading (all done sitting in a chair), in addition to their teaching, preaching, and other more "active" tasks. People who live inside their heads and never do any heavy lifting can still end up needing a prolonged rest leave from work. This is why it is good to have personal discipline about how much one works, how much one rests, and also how much one plays.

To Karl Barth we owe the observation that "a being is free only when it can determine and limit its activity." Barbara Brown Taylor, reflecting on this adage, laments that if this is so, she knows very few free beings. She adds, "I know people who can do five things at once who are incapable of doing nothing."[12] I must take exception to the notion that resting is "nothing." In fact, resting is intentionally doing something; it is not just the absence of activity.

Resting every day is not merely mandatory for human beings' health; a biblical concept of resting ought to have something to do with *shalom* — a term that all too often is translated "peace," but really means something more like "being well" or "being whole." Our problem is that we tend to associate peace, like rest, with the absence of activity, when in fact *shalom* more often than not involves the presence of God in our lives, when the God of all peace is with us.

Since resting is not optional for us, we need a better theology of rest. One of the most interesting facets about Jewish Sabbath theology is that the very first thing God ever hallowed, set apart, or deemed holy was the seventh day, the Sabbath. Christians tend to hallow the Lord's Day, and they understandably mix it up with the Sabbath in this regard. "There is evidence that for a very little while, early Christians tried to observe both the Sabbath and the resurrection on Sunday. Then the church and the synagogue got a nasty divorce and part of the separation agreement was the division of holy days."[13]

Certainly the earliest Christians, who were all Jews, observed both days, and there is no reason why the theological principle

12. B. Brown Taylor, *An Altar in the World: A Geography of Faith* (New York: HarperOne, 2009), p. 125. She quotes Barth without footnoting the source.

13. Taylor, *An Altar in the World*, pp. 128-29.

that undergirds this practice can't be adopted and adapted by us. We need a holy day to focus on worshiping the Lord. We also need seasons of rest, every week, indeed every day (and I don't just mean sleeping). We all need to have our own personal cycles of work, rest, sleep, and also play. And different persons will need more or less of each of these.

Since worship is also a non-negotiable for a Christian, it is best to figure worship into the cycle of rest and play (not, please, into the sleep cycle). In fact, every human body (indeed, every plant and animal body as well) has circadian rhythms, by which I do not just mean our sleep cycle. The word *circadian* actually means "around the day," and it refers to the cycles of our being awake as well as our sleeping. These rhythms are something human beings share with all other living beings, but more importantly, according to the story of beginnings, they are something we share with God. God "ceased" and admired his creative handiwork, and so should we, taking time to stop and smell the roses. Brian Edgar has suggested in a recent article that play can be and should be a part of worship. He points to music and dance within worship (Exod. 15:20) or a play within worship as examples of how they can and should overlap. This is worth thinking about. Furthermore, Edgar is right to point out that because play is not "serious" it tends to be undervalued both theologically and ethically. The problem is that play has been envisioned within the context of work, and not just any kind of work, but work that is done not as a calling but as a necessity, as something done to make money. In this scenario, Edgar acutely observes, if work is the spirit of capitalism, then play is the spirit of consumerism. It is seen as something that is "for me" and as an escape from the drudgery and necessity of work. This misevaluates both play and work from a theological point of view.[14]

14. The author has kindly allowed me to read this article, which in due course will be published in the *Dictionary of Scripture and Ethics*, edited by J. B. Green for Baker Books.

Sadly, America is not the land it was when Alexis de Tocqueville visited around 1840 and observed how very different Sunday was in America than it was in Europe. He remarked, "Not only have all ceased to work, but they appear to have ceased to exist."[15] Alas, it is no longer so. My humble suggestion would be that Christians need to take their weekends back from where they have been exiled to — the soccer fields, the malls, and of course, the workplace. If they want some freedom, then they need to know how to limit their activities, as Barth suggested. Christians need to do a better job of saying no. If a whole weekend without work is too much to expect, then follow Barbara Brown Taylor's suggestion about taking mini-sabbaths all during the week — a few hours here, there, and yonder. Now, when the Land of Opportunity is busily becoming the Land of Unemployment, is the time when we need to get our mental houses in order about the relationship of work and rest and play.

I would argue that, in principle, weekends should not be work time, but rather be worship time, rest time, sleep time, family time, visiting time, and play time. And so here would be a good place to say more about a theology of play. Too few persons have reflected meaningfully about a theology of play, but Jürgen Moltmann has done so, and it will behoove us to think along with him for a bit.

A Theology of Play and Work

Somewhere along the line, people have gotten the notion that not just dour Christians, but their God as well, are all work and no play, a real killjoy. Moltmann sets out to disprove this theory. Like the concept of "rest" or even "vacation," the idea of "play" has

15. A. de Tocqueville, *Democracy in America*, vol. 2 (New York: Colonial, 1899), p. 355.

been seen as something of an antonym — or could it be an antidote? — to work. Play does not have to do with vocation or calling, on this view, unless of course one is a professional player of some sort.

I would suggest that just as God rested and took delight in what he created, enjoying what he had made, it is possible to talk about "play" as a theological category. One of the clues that play may be a proper theological category is that clearly God has a sense of humor. Just look at some of the things he created — the duck-billed platypus, the pelican, the giraffe, the flamingo. These creatures are meant to produce a smile and a giggle by the very way they look. But only human beings apparently are laughing, because humor is a human thing.

But is play only a human thing? It would appear not. I have watched my cats have a ball chasing each other around the house, or even chasing their own tails, and then of course there are dogs playing endless games of fetch.

In some regards, as Moltmann points out, we have to ask about the ethics of play. For example, is it right to be playing games when innocent Christian men, women, and children are being raped, tortured, and killed in Darfur? It is Moltmann's thesis that "it is possible that in playing we can anticipate our liberation and with laughing rid ourselves of the bonds which alienate us from real life."[16]

Play is a form of celebration of life, and as such it celebrates in advance the joy, excitement, re-creation of the new creation. How appropriate that recreation, as we call it, emblemizes and celebrates in advance the time of re-creation. In such terms, then, play is not the antidote to work, but rather the recognition that there is so much more to life than just work, as in the old adage, "All work and no play makes Jack a dull boy." And play in the form of team

16. J. Moltmann, *A Theology of Play* (New York: Harper, 1972), p. 3. Hereafter page references to this book will be given parenthetically in the text.

games also emblemizes community, working together, striving for a common goal, achieving a worthwhile purpose.

As Moltmann points out, games tend to seem useless to those who are not participating in them, rather than to those that are. "Just asking for the purpose of a game makes a person a spoil-sport" (pp. 5-6). This is rather like the person who looks at a great work of art and has to say, "But what's the point?" If you have to ask, then you've missed the point.

Some people see games as an "escape" from the real world, and there is an element of truth in that. But play serves a variety of purposes — respite from the real world is but one of them; recreation, restoration, and renewal of hope are others. For example, when I watched my beloved Red Sox finally win the World Series in 2004 after more than eighty years of "keeping hope alive," I felt like all kinds of things were possible. In fact, in 2008 when the Celtics won the NBA championship, Kevin Garnett, an all-star player who had been on bad teams throughout his career, exulted, saying, "Anything is possible!" The tragedy and triumphs in small scale on the playing field give people hope that if such things can happen for underdogs on the court or playing field, then surely they can happen on a larger scale in life as well. The psychology of good games gives hope. This was never more clear than in the Beijing Olympic Games in the summer of 2008. Here, for a few moments, the world seemed united in playing its games. The Olympic Games present us with an almost eschatological vision of a world united, even if only for a few days. In short, games fuel the psychology of hope.

Of course, it is true that games have been used by governments as a distraction from the drudgery and darkness of real life, especially when "man's labor alienates and empties him" (p. 6). Games can be used by governments as prophylactics against revolution. "So every repressive regime must from time to time provide safety valves to release pent-up pressures of aggression it has caused and to keep the barrel from bursting" (p. 7). But that is but one use of games and, I would argue, not their main purpose or focus. When games are but an opiate for the masses, who have no other release, nothing else to look forward to in a culture and life full of regimentation and precious little freedom, it is easy to see why some would sneer at "mere games" as cynical distractions or at best compensations for the lack of joy and freedom in real life.

We have all met persons who are incapable of play, incapable of a real vacation, and who insist that they must be "doing something" even when on vacation. I once drove to a beautiful beach with a friend. The drive took hours. I was looking forward to swimming a bit, and just sitting on the beach and relaxing and taking in the beauty. But only a very short time after we got there and were sitting on the beach my friend turned to me and said, "Well, this is nice — what's next?" This is not what I would call "a sense of adventure." It is, rather, bringing a work mentality to play, and thus spoiling one of the major purposes of play and vacation — time that is not structured according to a work schedule! As Moltmann puts it, "Leisure then becomes a continuation of the rhythm of work by other means" (p. 9). This is a sort of destroying of the freedom that comes when we can set aside our work schedules for a while. "Games become hopeless and witless if they serve only to help us forget for a while what we cannot change anyway" (p. 12).

The Puritans used to scold their children by saying, "You have not come into this world for pleasure." But that is a part of the Puritan work ethic that is well left behind. I would not take us back to the world of either Prometheus with all his labors or the world of the Puritans with theirs. Neither, in fact, brought in the Kingdom of God. No matter how hard we try to squelch the freedom that comes with play, it will crop up again, even in the circles of the most poor — stick ball in the streets of New York, soccer in a dirty field outside a poor village in Afghanistan. It appears that God made us for play, as well as work, and children have a stronger sense of this than most adults do. Perhaps this is an area of life where the workaholics could learn how "a little child shall lead them." Even some high-intensity corporations are realizing these days that fostering play, even in the midst of work, serves the end of more content and more productive workers. It leads to the realization that work is not only not the curse but also not the be-all and end-all of human existence, and so play should not be seen as the enemy of work, the antithesis of work. Work, rest, play all have their places. Play is different from rest in that it of course involves activity, even vigorous activity, which is not the case with rest.

Play at its best is prospective, while rest is retrospective. God looked back at his good week's work and rested. What I mean by saying play is prospective is that in play we are foreshadowing the future, or as Moltmann playfully puts it, "we are increasingly playing with the future in order to get to know it" (p. 13). Oddly enough, this is close to how future prophecy works as well: "They will beat their swords into plowshares and their spears into pruning hooks. Nation will not take up sword against nation, nor will they train for war anymore. Everyone will sit under their own vine and under their own fig tree and no one will make them afraid" (Mic. 4:3-4). Just as war games foreshadow and prepare people for the future, so normal games do as well. Normal games give a foretaste for what we hope for; war games sadly do the opposite, getting us ramped up for what we dread and usually desire to avoid.

Moltmann, interestingly enough, begins his proper discussion of play by starting with creation and asking the old question, "Why is there something rather than nothing?" That is, why did God create the universe, if God is a free and self-sufficient being? This is a very fair question, and Moltmann finds an answer in Proverbs 8:30, where the Wisdom of God says, "I was daily his delight, rejoicing before him always." Moltmann says, "This is the wisdom of creation. It does not take the world and life either more seriously or more lightly than creation demands, a creation which is neither divine nor anti-divine. Not Atlas carrying the world on his shoulders, but the child is holding the globe in his hands" (p. 16).

Could God have created the world, with all its curious creatures, for his pure pleasure? Could he have put the ball in play, so to speak, out of joy unspeakable, saying "what fun!"? Did God approach the creation with the imagination and excitement of an artist desiring to create something good, and true, and beautiful, and enjoyable, and fun. A universe where there is a measure of play as well as fair play? A universe that has potential and some freedom of self-expression? Suppose play and games remind us of the original creation intent and character of the Creator, as well as foreshadowing where this giant soap opera is all heading?

Creation, as it turns out, has something in common with play — the activity is meaningful, but not necessary. God didn't need to create the universe, any more than I need to go play a game of basketball. Neither is *necessary* in the basic meaning of that word. But God's playing and ours differ in that God can create something out of nothing, which brings God delight, enjoyment. "Man can only play with something, which in turn, is playing with him. When man is playing, he is himself at stake in the game and he is also being played with. He cannot play with nothing or a void. He can only play in love" (pp. 17-18). Or, as I would prefer to put it, he can only play in relationship to other people or things. Humans are not self-sufficient beings, unlike God. Still,

> like the creation, man's games are an expression of freedom, not caprice, for playing relates to the joy of the Creator with his creation and the pleasure of the player with his game. Like creation, games combine sincerity and mirth, suspense and relaxation. The player is wholly absorbed in his game and takes it seriously, yet at the same time he transcends himself and his game, for it is after all a game. So he is realizing his freedom without losing it. He steps outside of himself without selling himself. The symbol of the world as God's free creation out of his good pleasure corresponds to the symbol of man as the child of God. (p. 18)

And if we are always the children of God, then it follows from this that we should always enjoy our play, as well as our rest and work. What if human beings were all created in joy, and for joy? What if enjoying God and his creation forever is part of why we were created in the first place? What if settling for happiness in life is falling far short of the joy we were created for in the first place? What if the creation mandate to fill and subdue, to tend and to care for, did not come with the harsh reprimand, "Be good for something, or you are good for nothing"? What if instead our work and our doing were understood in the larger context of joy and of play? What if we were made to whistle while we work, not merely enjoying the work, but remembering that we are more than our work, greater than our tasks, created in the image of a joyful God?

What if the one who said, "I came that you might have life, and have it abundantly," really was the Incarnation of God, and revealed God's inner nature? What if God's *joie de vivre* is something he wants us to have as well? Moltmann says, "The glorification of God lies in the demonstrative joy of existence. Then man in his uninhibited fondness for this finite life and by his affirmation of mortal beauty shares the infinite pleasure of the Creator" (p. 21). There is something about play, as more than a respite from work, that reminds us that we are not just all about doing and working. We are also about being and celebrating existence, and laughing at ourselves. "Earthbound labor finds relief in rejoicing, dancing, singing, and playing. This also does labor a lot of good" (p. 24). And there is something as well to be said for the notion that watching graceful athletes serves to remind us of God's grace, not just human gifts and skills. Play presents us with various cameos of the character of God when it is done well.

One of the things play and games remind us of is that startling reversals can happen in life: the last can become first. Just this past year, baseball fans marveled at the story of the Tampa Bay Rays, a true worst-to-first story. And Jesus is the paradigmatic storyteller when it comes to tales of dramatic reversal. We cannot read the parables without recognizing that Jesus had a sense of humor and a sense of play. To imagine the camel trying to do the limbo through the eye of a needle is to realize that even the serious business of entering the Kingdom has its comical and playful side.

But for the Christian worker, Easter's resurrection is the ultimate emblem of reversal, the ultimate laughing at the power of death. As Moltmann says, "Here indeed begins the laughing of the redeemed, the dancing of the liberated, and the creative game of new, concrete concomitants of the liberty which has been opened for us, even if we still live under conditions with little cause for rejoicing" (p. 29).

The Christian at play can push the limits of physical endurance in a game, or in the game of life, and know there will be a sequel without equal. There will always be another time of play, in the Kingdom, because life has swallowed up death in the person of Jesus. The Christian can rejoice and play the game of new creation, knowing it has already begun to happen in Christ, and one day we shall be like him. There is a special freedom in knowing that God is in control of the game, and he has promised it will turn out with a joyful ending. Moltmann puts it this way: "Life is not a struggle but pre-play, not preparatory labor but prevision of the future life of rejoicing" (p. 35).

It is God in Christ who will bring the end of all things we now know and bring in the new creation, and this is Good News because it means new creation will not be a human achievement or accomplishment. It will not be accomplished by human work. Indeed, play and celebration are closer to the character of new creation in some respects than work, for they better capture the spirit of new creation, the joy, than our current work normally does. When Christ the bridegroom returns, his bride will be waiting, and they will dance and celebrate and rejoice and play. This is not to say I am taking back what I said earlier about there being work to be done in the Kingdom. As Moltmann warns:

Christian eschatology has never thought of the end of history as a kind of retirement or payday or accomplished purpose but has regarded it totally without purpose as a hymn of praise for unending joy, as an ever-varying round dance of the redeemed in the Trinitarian fullness of God, and as the complete harmony of soul and body. It has not hoped for an unearthly heaven of bodyless souls but for a new body penetrated by the spirit and redeemed from the bondage of law and death. . . . Christian eschatology has painted the end of history in the colors of aesthetic categories. (p. 34)

This is quite correct, and if the endgame looks like that, then there are good and bad ways to play along the way: there is playing that foreshadows the endgame, and there is play that does not. This is why, in the end, Moltmann exhorts, "Play should liberate, not tranquilize, awaken, not anesthetize. Liberating play is protest against the evil plays of the oppressor and the exploiter. Therefore, play seriously and fight joyously" (p. 113). Play, then, from a theological point of view, is not supposed to be the opiate of the masses, something that stupefies; rather, it is supposed to be a foretaste of glory divine, a preview of coming attractions, a gift to us that reminds us of the gift Who keeps on giving — Christ the risen one.

In the nexus of work, rest, and play, maintaining a creative balance, like a ballerina on her toes, we dance back and forth among these three poles, realizing we have not merely been saved to serve and for good works; we have been saved to rejoice in the freedom we have to be mini-creators like God, and, yes, we have been saved to relax and appreciate what we have accomplished at the end of a long week. Neither work nor rest nor play alone should define us or confine us. We are not merely what we do or what we abstain from doing. We are created in the image of God and re-created in the image of Christ, and that is God the worker's, God the lover's doing on our behalf. This means we can see life and its activities and resting places as a gift from God, and our identities can be primarily found in whose we are, not merely what we do or abstain from. It was Jesus who said that unless we turn and become as a child again, we cannot enter the Kingdom of God; and among other things that means we need once more to learn how to play as blissfully, creatively, and obliviously as a child. And oddly enough, when we are doing this, we image forth the Creator who made all these odd and wonderful creatures great and small — and took delight and joy from doing so.

And one more thing. Caught up in the nexus between work and rest and play, we come to learn in each of these states that life is a gift, and if we play it like the Giver, with reverence, with respect, worshiping the Giver rather than the gift and the work it produces, then we have truly completed the lifecycle for which we were all intended — caught up in love and wonder and joy and praise of our Maker. Let the play begin!

Take This Job and . . .

All language about the future, as any economist or politician
will tell you, is simply a set of signposts pointing into a fog.

N. T. Wright

In his profound and frank reflections on work, Miroslav Volf
points out that the postmodern, Western obsession with work is
more a result of the preoccupation with self-realization and au-
thentication than a result of some long-forgotten Protestant work
ethic. I think he is largely right about this, for the narcissistic preoccupation with self-realization and being a self-made man or
woman requires doing and making. It requires work. "The contemporary religion of work has little to do either with worship of
God or with God's demands on human life; it has to do with 'worship' of self and human demands on the self."[1]

The question we should be asking ourselves honestly is this: Is
my sense of identity so bound up in what I do that I have become a
compulsive workaholic just to validate my existence and give myself a sense of importance, worth, and value? If we can plead guilty

---

1. M. Volf, *Work in the Spirit: Toward a Theology of Work* (Eugene: Wipf
and Stock, 2001), p. 129.

to this charge, then it is clear that what we need in our lives is not merely a more biblical sense and understanding of work, but a biblical understanding of self as well. We are not merely what we do, for we were created in the image of God as beings of sacred worth and renewed in the image of Christ by grace through faith — and neither of these truths has anything to do with our work or workload. We are defined by our relationship with God, and our humanity is grounded in that relationship. We are *imago dei*, not *homo faber* as Karl Marx once claimed. We are neither self-made humans nor work-made humans. Our work does not bestow on us our humanity, but it is the way we can express in a useful manner our likeness to God as creators, sustainers, redeemers.

One of the keys to having a truly Christian perspective on work is recognizing that what we do is part of who we are. And if the Spirit is shaping our character, then what we do must reflect the fruit of the Spirit. Whatever cannot be done in accordance with love, joy, peace, patience, kindness, goodness, gentleness, and self-control probably shouldn't be done at all, and if it is done, it needs to be recognized as being a crisis response to a fallen situation, not God's highest and best for us. While it can certainly be argued and should be realized that there are "lesser of two evils" situations in this world, this should not cause us to change our basic definition of good work or the goal to do all things in a way that fulfills the Great Commandment and the Great Commission, glorifying God and edifying human beings. Let me give you an example, but one with pathos involved.

A mother of three is pregnant with a fourth child. When she begins experiencing unusual pain, she goes to her doctor for an ultrasound and learns that the pregnancy is ectopic. In an ectopic pregnancy, which involves the fertilized egg implanting outside the uterus, the mother's life is in serious danger, and there is almost no chance of the child surviving outside the womb for more than a very brief period of time. What should this mother and her husband do?

They pray hard, consult with their priest, seek the counsel of friends, but the clock is running out. A decision must be made. Weighing heavily on the mother's mind is that if she chooses to carry the child to term and then dies on the operating table, she will be depriving her three girls of their mother and her husband of his wife, which seems an inhuman and inhumane and even selfish thing to do, just on the off chance that her fourth child will survive birth for a few days or weeks.

The mother is a pro-life Catholic and is deeply conflicted on this matter. Can she say it is absolutely necessary that she get an abortion to remedy this situation? No, she cannot say that with absolute certainty. She *may* survive the surgical delivery and go on to live a good life, but the odds are truly not good. So, she must make a decision based on faith, not absolute certainty. In the end, the mother decides, with great tears, to have the abortion, and then to pray for God's forgiveness if she has chosen poorly.

In a perfect world, women would not have ectopic pregnancies, but this is not the best of all possible worlds; it is a fallen one, and this affects the ethical choices that we make. But we seldom look at the abortion situation through the lens of the realities of human fallenness. Instead of saying that on the day this woman had her abortion a husband was spared from losing his wife and three children were spared from losing their mother, we choose to say the unborn child's life was taken.

But we do have such "lesser of two evils" choices to make in this world, and some of those choices will be work related. Consider, for a moment, the doctor who performed the abortion. Imagine him to be a Christian who is likewise caught in a terrible ethical dilemma of two bad choices. Picture him and the mother agreeing that they will pray and thank God for the gift of the life of this unborn child and offer it back to God, hoping and praying they have made the right decision to do the abortion.

The doctor, who has sworn to uphold the Hippocratic oath and to "do no harm," nonetheless feels guilty about this deed and prays for forgiveness from God. He does not want to be defined by means of this work as an "abortionist"; indeed, it is the only abortion he has ever performed in a lifetime of helping to heal and save lives. If he must be defined by his work in some large measure, he wishes to be known as a healer, and in this case as a person who rescued the life of a mother for her husband and family. The work that the doctor did on that day may well have been necessary work, a choice of the lesser of two evils, and so we must distinguish between all the work we may have to do in this life, and what is strictly speaking work from which we need not repent. Not everything we do in life can we do with clean hands and an absolutely certain heart.

In other words, while there may be a difference between good and godly work and the sum total of all work that of necessity must be done in this world to preserve the possibility of good and godly work, nevertheless we must not lose sight of the creation intent of making us caretakers of God's garden, or the eschatological goal of participation in the bringing in of God's final Kingdom on earth.

How, then, do we discern the proper boundaries for our work, so that we do not seek to find our identity in work, nor lose ourselves in our work, nor become workaholics? My answer to this question is simple — an adequate amount of rest, play, and worship provides the boundaries for work and the reminders that work is not the be-all and end-all of our existence. Each person, no doubt, will have a different necessary proportion when it comes to work, rest, play, and worship, but one must find that balance. It should not be just a balance between work and rest, or just a balance between worship and work, or just a balance between play and work, but should involve some of all of these things.

Worship is indeed of paramount importance for our well-being and spiritual life and growth and should be given definite priority in our lives, but play and rest are also necessary to our very beings, not to mention our being productive workers. My suggestion is that for Christians Sunday should be for worship, family, and play, and Saturday for rest, but also during the week there should be time for rest and for some play. Under the rubric of play I include any and all physical exercise as well. And if all of this is done unto God's glory and in praise of our Maker, then all of it is doxology.

Though we live in a world where lots of people talk about and long for retirement, in fact the truth is that most contemporary human beings have far less leisure time than those living in the Middle Ages in Europe. Even peasants got to take part in the holy days and festivals of Christian Europe, which took up more than a third of the yearly calendar. The holy days were the holidays, and they were nicely spread out during the year. We are a long way from that today.

In the 1960s, in the heyday of belief in "progress" through work and technological advancement, it was once suggested to a U.S. Senate hearing that by 1985 people could be working just 22-27 hours a week, and many would be able to retire at 38![2] These calculations would be laughable if they weren't made in earnest, reflecting an earnest and naïve belief in the human capacity to re-make the world, the workplace, and ourselves. Alas, a survey in 1990 showed that between 1973 and 1990 the actual amount of leisure enjoyed by the average American worker shrunk by 37 percent, with the average work week rising from 41 to 47 hours a week. "In contemporary technological civilization, which can boast of remarkable labor-saving innovations, human beings paradoxically work more than they have ever worked before!"[3] The labor-saving devices themselves paradoxically created more work.

Volf has perceptively commented on how our workaholic worldview leaks over into our play and rest and even into our worship lives. We insist now on more frenzied workouts, more "active" play, more "concentrated" rest, and, yes, more "lively"

2. See Volf, *Work in the Spirit*, p. 134.
3. Volf, *Work in the Spirit*, p. 135.

worship. Our vision of work spills over into our vision of how these other activities or conditions should be viewed or done.[4]

In an earlier book,[5] I looked at the nature of worship in the light of Kingdom come, and it is clear to me that all that we are and do must be doxological in character. As Romans 12:1-2 puts it, the very offering up of our selves and our activities to God is our logical worship. We serve and worship God through our work, if done rightly. This, however, does not exonerate us from the need to be involved every week in corporate worship so that we may commune, together with the body of Christ, with God. We need to have a time to enjoy and practice the presence of God corporately and not just individually. Our ordinary work, which individualizes us, is no substitute for corporate worship.

In worship we anticipate the dance, the celebration of the new creation, and remind ourselves where we are all heading, and why we are doing all these things in the first place. "When Christians commune with God in worship, they come to drink from that fountain their very life as Christians and hence their identity as human beings depends on. At the same time, in worship they anticipate the enjoyment of God in the new creation where they will communally dwell in the triune God and the triune God will dwell in them (see Rev. 21:22; John 17:21)."[6] The "rhythmic alternation between work and worship, labor and liturgy is one of the distinguishing features of a Christian's way of being-in-the world."[7] Worship is an anticipation of the eschaton, depicting the peace, communion, and community living in the presence of God we will experience there.[8]

4. Volf, *Work in the Spirit,* p. 135.

5. See *We Have Seen His Glory: A Kingdom Perspective on Worship* (Grand Rapids: Eerdmans, 2010).

6. Volf, *Work in the Spirit,* p. 137.

7. N. Wolterstorff, *Until Justice and Peace Embrace* (Grand Rapids: Eerdmans, 1987), p. 147.

8. See, rightly, Volf, *Work in the Spirit,* p. 140.

We have not had much occasion or opportunity in this study to reflect on the relationship of work to our ecosphere and environment, but clearly much more theological reflection needs to be done in this area. Obviously, war is the single largest destroyer of the earth and of human life (after disease), which is precisely why ethically we can debate whether it is ever work worth doing. More ethically ambiguous are professions that, while providing needed work and even, in some limited respects, needed products, nonetheless are very hazardous to the life and health of the workers and to the environment as well. I am referring, for example, to the mining of coal, and in particular the strip mining of the land, leaving huge slag heaps, which destroys whole regions of our beautiful mountains here in Kentucky where I live. Another example, of course, would be the growing of tobacco, a product no one needs, everyone should avoid, and most definitely is hazardous to the consumer's health.

It is precisely when we forget that we are natural beings, requiring air to breathe and clean water to drink and food from the good earth to eat in order to exist at all, that it becomes possible to talk about work in isolation from its effect on nature, or, worse, to justify any abuse of nature by way of the creation order mandate to fill the earth and subdue it. No doubt the dramatic population shift from farms to cities in the twentieth century has helped make possible a shift in thinking that allowed us to forget our dependence upon and connection with the land, including in our work and in our survival as a human species.

Part of the creation story involves Adam tending and caring for Eden. As we said before, the first profession seems to have been that of the gardener, according to the Bible. Thus, "protecting from ecological imbalance and irreversible damage is an important dimension of care for the nonhuman creation."[9] Sometimes the notion of "subduing" the earth has been taken to give us a li-

9. Volf, *Work in the Spirit*, p. 145.

cense to do as we would with wild nature, rather than realizing that our task is to set fallen creation free to do what God intended it to do in the first place. We can think of the matter this way: God created a big, beautiful world for us to live in, to enjoy, to play in, to worship in. Why would we want to destroy or irrevocably mar his masterpiece, just to satisfy a need we have, which could be satisfied without being so destructive of nature?

If "this is my Father's world," then we ought to treat it with the knowledge that it does not belong to us, just as growing up we were taught to treat other people's belongings with respect since they are not ours and we are therefore not free to do with them as we please. Furthermore, we must remember that we leave a footprint, a legacy, for our children to follow. Do we want to leave a larger carbon footprint or a smaller one? Do we wish to leave the world a better place for our offspring or a more devastated, polluted place?

There is in fact room for much more fruitful reflection on all the topics discussed in this book, but it is now time to sum up some of the crucial things we have learned along the way.

In Sum

First and foremost, it is the task of all human beings to love God with our whole heart and to love our neighbor as ourself. These tasks are "job one" for all those created in the image of God. Second, and more specifically for Christians, it is our honor to be tasked with making disciples of all nations. Any other tasks, jobs, or work we undertake must be seen as subheadings under these primary, lifelong tasks. This is why I have distinguished in this study between tasks we may spend most of our time doing in life, calling them the main tasks, and the tasks that are of primary importance for all believers. Our main work, whatever it is, should not be radically separated from our primary task in life, and it certainly shouldn't be at odds with the Prime Mandate.

Broadly speaking, the original mandate to humankind was to fill the earth and subdue it, to tend the garden and to care for it. There is not a lot of filling and subduing left to do anymore, quite frankly, but plenty of tending and caring for still required. Work done by those in the image of God should mirror the creative, sustaining, and redeeming work of God; indeed, it should be an attempt to be God's co-laborers in these enterprises, as we are not merely created in the image of God but are re-created in the image of Christ and are stewards of the mysteries of God. We must always keep steadily in view that work itself is not God's curse on humankind just as surely as it is not our salvation either. Work should neither be demonized nor divinized.

We talked a good deal about work as vocation and vocation as work, and distinguished between calling, gifting, vocation, and the work itself. The calling is not the gifting, nor is the gifting the vocation, nor is the vocation the work itself. We pointed out at length the problems with the Lutheran theology of vocation, but also with Miroslav Volf's theology of charism in relationship to work. We still need a theology of vocation and work. But our theology of vocation should have nothing to do with a theology of station or social standing in life, not least because plenty of Christians are born into or forced into horrible situations and relationships quite apart from their wills, and we should not assume that "whatever is, is right"; much less should we assume that "whatever is, is God's call on my life." The calling comes from God, and often calls us out from and away from the station, status, and sometimes even the relationships we find ourselves in when we become Christ's disciples.

God, however, does not merely call us; the Spirit of God gifts us to do specific tasks for the Kingdom, for the body of Christ, for our families, and for ourselves. We must listen for the calling and look for the leading of God. We must also not mistake the calling to be a Christian, which enables us to fulfill the Prime Mandate, with the calling to some specific human task. The two must be distinguished. In the course of a lifetime God may equip us and call us to various jobs or tasks. We should not assume that the initial call to be a carpenter, or a minister, or a doctor, is necessarily intended to be our lifelong vocation. We must be flexible and continue to listen to God's call on our lives.

We also spent some time discussing what counts as work. Marriage and family should not be defined as our work, though the roles of husband and wife and parent certainly involve work and various tasks. We must be able to distinguish between social conditions, relationships, and work. Paul, for instance, doesn't talk about being "called" or having a "vocation" to be married or single, or be a husband or a wife. He does, however, say that it requires a specific grace gift to remain single and celibate for the Lord, just as it requires a specific grace gift to be married in the Lord.

It is precisely Paul's eschatological and Kingdom viewpoint that allows him to suggest that marriage is simply a blessed option for Christians, no longer a creation order mandate. This is one of the tell-tale signs that shows us that our Christian theology of work cannot simply come out of reflection on a theology of creation and the creation order mandate. Likewise, Jesus makes clear in texts such as Mark 10 that marriage is something in which God draws two people together, but it is only for "those to whom it is given." We should not assume it is for everyone, in the light of the coming Kingdom of God. In the Kingdom, we do things because we have been graced and gifted and called to do them, not simply because we are capable of doing them and might even be good at them. In addition, there is very little good and godly work that should necessarily be deemed gender-specific, or a man's task as opposed to a woman's task. The Holy Spirit, not gender, determines who gets what gifts and what one is graced and called to do.

I have also stressed that we need to have a teleological sense about our work, that is, a good sense of the Kingdom ends it serves, what its aims and purposes are, what lasting good it may do. How does our work foreshadow, prepare for, provide a foretaste of what is to come, when we will study war no more and when swords will be turned into plowshares? These are the sorts of questions we should ask, when the issue arises about to what sorts of tasks Christians should devote their lives. What will be your legacy, and how would you want your life work to be assessed by God and his people? Do you long for nothing more than the approbation of the One who can say on the last day, "Well done, good and faithful servant, inherit the Kingdom"?

We talked at some length about the theology of the priesthood of all believers and the hallowing of all good and godly tasks. The division of work into sacred and secular tasks and the notion that only those called to specifically "religious" tasks are actually "called to ministry" by God are not well-grounded biblical ideas. To the contrary, all tasks should be done to the glory of God and for the edification of human beings, and we are all called to offer ourselves up to God as living sacrifices, as our logical worship or faithful service.

We also spent considerable time talking about the relationship of work to rest, and of work to play, and of work to worship, and about the need for a proper balance of all these things in a normal Christian life. We also discussed the relationship of work to art and to works of art. In my view, art is a means of fulfilling the creation order mandate to be creative as God is creative.

We spent an entire chapter dialoguing with Andy Crouch about the need to see our work as culture making. Too often Christians have had too individualistic, privatistic, pragmatic a view of the ends and aims of good work — as a means of surviving, of obtaining a paycheck, or of supporting a family. While these purely functional views of work are true as far as they go, they are insufficient. Most of us have been in the place of doing work we were ill-suited for, work that we despised and wanted to quit, singing that old country tune, "Take this job and shove it. . . ." But work was intended to be so much more in the vision of

God and in light of the Kingdom. Blessed are those who find and follow God's calling in their lives to their own good and godly tasks. Too few Christians have realized that our work is not merely our means of support but also our means of making a difference in the world, indeed our means of culture making. Crouch calls us not merely to transform culture by our work, but also to learn to be creative enough in what we do to be actual creators of culture, not merely imitators, critiquers, transformers, or even demolition experts when it comes to extant culture. Our work shapes us; the question is, will we fashion it into something that reflects our glorious Creator and the primary tasks for which we exist?

As I mentioned earlier in this book, recently I was visiting the grounds of the new Billy Graham Library in Charlotte, North Carolina, and I found the stone erected in memory of Ruth Graham, Billy's wife. It said, "Construction Completed: Thanks for Your Patience." Perhaps, in the end, we may take comfort in the fact that all along God the Worker has been working on and in us to bring us to perfection, even as we have been busy working out our vocation and indeed our salvation with fear and trembling.

At the end of the day we need to trust the potter, who keeps molding and remolding us in his image. If we focus too much and too closely on the pot and its functions, all we will notice is the flaws and cracks in the vessel. Thank goodness there is the treasure of God's living presence placed in our lives: "But we have this treasure in clay jars, so that it may be made clear that this extraordinary power belongs to God and does not come from us. . . . So we do not lose heart. Even though our outer nature is wasting away, our inner nature is being renewed day by day" (2 Cor. 4:7, 16).

Soli Deo Gloria.